RELIGI
PERSONAL LIFE

Debating ethics and faith with leading thinkers and public figures including:

ALASTAIR CAMPBELL,
STEVE CHALKE,
DELIA SMITH,

Polly Toynbee, Giles Fraser,
John Harris, Mary Ann Sieghart

Edited by **LINDA WOODHEAD** with **NORMAN WINTER**

Commentary by **CHARLES CLARKE**

DARTON · LONGMAN + TODD

First published in 2013 by
Darton, Longman and Todd Ltd
1 Spencer Court
140 – 142 Wandsworth High Street
London SW18 4JJ

ISBN 978-0-232-53018-6

A catalogue record for this book is available from the British Library.

Phototypeset by Judy Linard
Printed and bound in Great Britain by Bell and Bain, Glasgow

Contents

Introduction

This book is based on the Westminster Faith Debates of 2013. The series covered the theme of religion and personal life, and invited leading figures to debate some of the most controversial topics of the day, including abortion, same-sex marriage and euthanasia.

The debates attracted a great deal of interest and media coverage, and we received many requests to make them available in print. This is the result. It presents the best of the series in a condensed form, together with additional research findings and teaching materials. We offer new commentary and reflection in every chapter to draw out the most important themes and conclusions.

THE DEBATES

Behind the book lies a series of debates about religion which was initiated by Charles Clarke[1] and Linda Woodhead[2] in 2012 and quickly grew to become a focus of public and media interest.

The first series of the Westminster Faith Debates dealt with the place of religion and public life. The second series, which feeds this book, deals with the complementary theme of religion and personal life. It follows the course of a human life, beginning with birth and ending

[1] The Rt Hon. Charles Clarke was Labour MP for Norwich South from 1997 until 2010. He was Education Secretary from 2002 to 2004 and Home Secretary from 2004 to 2006 in the government led by Tony Blair. He is currently Visiting Professor in Politics and Faith at Lancaster University, and Visiting Professor in Politics at the University of East Anglia.

[2] Linda Woodhead MBE, DD is Professor of Sociology of Religion at Lancaster University. She was Director of the AHRC/ESRC Religion and Society Programme between 2007 and 2013. Her research looks at what is happening to religion across the world, and she is interested in what religious people really think. Her books include *Everyday Lived Islam in Europe* (Ashgate, 2013), *The Spiritual Revolution* (with Paul Heelas, Blackwell, 2005), and *A Very Short Introduction to Christianity* (Oxford University Press, 2004).

with death, and debating the difficult issues to be faced along the way.

As their name suggests, the Faith Debates are staged in central London each year, and attract a large audience from Westminster, Whitehall and elsewhere. Their purpose is to bring the best research on religion into public debate. They are funded by the Arts and Humanities Research Council, the Economic and Social Research Council, and Lancaster University.

Each debate is chaired and introduced by Charles and Linda, and involves a panel of expert speakers. Panels are selected to include as broad a range of views as possible. They include religious and non-religious views, and a range of political opinion. Contributors are academics, politicians, journalists and other public figures, and members of various faith groups. What they have in common is that they have thought long and hard about the topic under discussion and have an informed opinion to present. After giving a short statement of their position, they enter into debate with one another and with the audience.

THE SURVEY – ETHICAL OPINION IN BRITAIN TODAY

This series of debates was supported by a survey which was specially commissioned to inform them. It offers a new understanding of the breadth of opinion on issues of personal morality in Great Britain, and allows us to take the moral temperature of the nation.

The poll was designed by Linda Woodhead and administered by YouGov. It was completed online in January 2013 by 4,437 people, and covers England, Wales and Scotland. It is representative of all GB adults aged 18+, and includes people who identify with all the major religions represented in Britain (some of the sample sizes were boosted to ensure adequate representation). It was analysed by Linda and Bernard Silverman, Professor of Statistics at Oxford University.

One of the unique features of the survey is that it asks about all the main dimensions of religion, including beliefs, commitments, belongings, identity, public practices, personal practices and sources of guidance and authority. This makes it possible, for the first time, to find out what religious people of various kinds really think about the whole range of moral issues covered in the debates.

A key finding is that most religious people have similar opinions to the population as a whole. This is perhaps not surprising, given that religious people make up about two-thirds of the population of GB (here, as in the rest of the book, 'religious people' means those who say that they have a religion, that they are Anglican, Catholic, Muslim, Hindu etc.). But it had often been assumed that religious people are much more conservative on issues of personal morality than non-religious people (non-religious means those who say they have 'no religion'). We know now that this is not the case. Most religious people are liberal – in the sense that they believe that individuals should be free to make decisions about the things which deeply affect their own life.

So where does the view that religious people are conservative or, more accurately, 'authoritarian or communitarian' on matters of personal morality come from? (Authoritarian or communitarian here means believing that the individual should be guided by higher authorities and/ or the views and interests of a community rather than merely by his or her own judgement.)

In part it comes from the official teachings of faith groups, upheld by their leaders. The Catholic Church is officially opposed to abortion, same-sex marriage and euthanasia, for example, and the Church of England (Anglican) is officially opposed to same-sex marriage. As our poll shows, however, this does not mean that the majority of people who call themselves Catholic or Anglican agree. The survey uncovered a major gap between what religious leaders say and what religious people today actually believe. It also shows that there is a wide 'values gap' between where the major churches are on these issues and where the general population is.

Nevertheless, religious people do not all share the same views, any more than the population as a whole does. What we find is a minority of people in Great Britain who have conservative views on issues of personal morality, views which are at variance with those of the wider population.

The survey allows us to gauge the nature and strength of this 'moral minority' for the first time. It finds that 8.5% of the population oppose the more liberal attitudes of the 'moral majority', a majority which represents 91.5% of the population. The three issues on which the moral minority are most clearly at variance with the majority are abortion, same-sex marriage and euthanasia. They would like to ban abortion or lower the time limit on abortions, they do not believe that same-sex marriage should be lawful, and they do not think that the current law which makes helping someone to die a criminal offence should be changed.

Most people in the moral minority are religious, but the interesting finding is that 45% of them are 'strictly religious'. By this we mean that they believe with certainty that there is a God and they take their main authority from God, scripture or religious teachings. These 'Godfearers' are a minority in all religions, but are most likely to be Muslim, Baptist or Roman Catholic – in that order.

While being strictly religious is the single most important predictor of whether you hold the views of the moral minority, the survey finds that there are other factors which count in relation to certain issues. For example, men are more likely than women to take a narrow, more conservative view of what counts as a family, and older people are much more likely to be hostile to same-sex marriage than younger ones.

Overall, it is interesting to see how little our views on personal morality seem to be shaped by factors such as gender, religion, class, ethnicity, education and political views. The fact that someone belongs to this or that political party, for example, does not allow you to read off what their views will be on issues of personal morality. Nor does the fact that they are Hindu, Anglican or any other religious affiliation. The only thing which has a striking effect on ethical views is being strictly religious. In other words, it seems that we really do make up our own minds about these issues, rather than being swayed by groups we identify with, our particular social situations, or even our political commitments.

The significant amount of consensus in public opinion on most of the issues debated in this book counts against the idea that there is a major lack of cohesion in Britain and a breakdown of cultural agreement. When it comes to the big decisions which we have to face in our own lives or those of people we know, many people share a common moral vision and agree on some basic principles. Central among these are fairness (not discriminating against people, in the sense of treating some worse than others), and liberty (the belief that when it comes to decisions which concern our own lives and bodies very directly, each person should be free to make his or her own decisions).

Even on the three issues that are most controversial in our series of six, we find a degree of consensus, as Figure 1 shows, although there is more agreement over some issues than others – more over assisted dying than over same-sex marriage, for example.

	Liberal	Intermediate	Authoritarian/ communitarian	Don't know
1. Abortion	**Raise or keep current time limit**	**Lower current time limit**	**Ban abortions**	**Don't know**
Religious people	43%	30%	9%	18%
General population	46%	28%	7%	19%
2. Same-sex marriage	**Allow**	**N/A**	**Don't allow**	**Don't know**
Religious people	43%	N/A	43%	14%
General population	53%	N/A	34%	14%
3. Assisted dying	**Allow**	**N/A**	**Don't allow**	**Don't know**
Religious people	64%	N/A	21%	14%
General population	70%	N/A	16%	14%

Figure 1: Views of the GB population on abortion, same-sex marriage and assisted dying

What this table also hints at, and the debates make very clear, is that popular opinion and legislation are not always in step. The discrepancy is clearest on euthanasia, where a very large majority are in favour of allowing it under certain circumstances, but the law disallows it. On some issues the law follows public opinion quite closely (as it seems to be doing on same-sex marriage), and on others it is distant from it (as on assisted dying).

Opinion also changes over time. On same-sex marriage, for example, the survey shows that each generation has become considerably more liberal than the previous one. Change does not always go in a liberal direction – new generations may become more conservative on some issues (for example, older people a little more likely to be in favour of assisted dying than younger ones), but on most issues the direction of travel has been in a liberalising direction.

But although public opinion has tended to become more liberal in recent decades, religious opinion – most especially that of religious leaders and the 'Godfearers' – has changed less quickly. As a result, the gap between official religious opinion and public opinion has widened considerably. On some issues, as in their strong opposition to same-sex marriage, most religious leaders are now hostile to majority opinion as well as to new legislation. Both the survey and the debates highlight this disagreement, and explore what is at stake.

THE BOOK

Each chapter of this book offers a summary version of one of the Faith Debates. It presents the original words of the speakers, and is based on recordings and transcripts of what they said. These have been edited and condensed by Linda Woodhead and Norman Winter, a former radio producer with BBC Radio 4. Speakers have had a chance to check, and in some cases changes have been made for the sake of clarity and flow.

Charles Clarke opens each chapter with a personal reflection on the debate, written for the book. Linda then offers an opening discussion of public opinion on the issue in question. The chapters end with short summaries of each debate written by Linda, a sample of media reaction, and some suggested follow-up resources.

The debates are available to watch or listen to online, or listen to in full, at www.faith debates.org.uk (or simply google Faith Debates). There you will also find a full listing of media coverage, the full survey results, and the press releases prepared for each debate.

The debates originally grew out of a £12m national research investment called 'Religion and Society' which was directed by Linda Woodhead. More details of the research projects involved and their findings can be found at www.religionandsociety.org.uk (or simply google Religion and Society.

The purpose of the book, as of the debates, is to present reliable research, offer the best possible articulations of a range of different views, and help people review their own positions and make up their own minds.

Each chapter offers a snapshot of the current interplay between public opinion, religious opinion, and legislation on the issue in question. Some of the participants are politicians pushing for a change in legislation, some are religious leaders and theologians, some are atheists and opponents of religion, and some are people active in professions like medicine, teaching and journalism. They all have something important to say, and they all want to convince you that they are right – but not all of them can be!

Our purpose isn't to tell you what to think, or merely to reflect public opinion: it is to inform and shape an ongoing debate. We hope that you will enjoy being part of the conversation, and that listening to the arguments will help clarify your own views on these sensitive topics which touch us all.

Linda Woodhead
Lancaster

Acknowledgements

The Faith Debates were devised by Charles Clarke and Linda Woodhead. They are generously supported by the Arts and Humanities Research Council and the Economic and Social Research Council and Lancaster University. Professor Tony McEnery at Lancaster University has been a staunch supporter throughout, and we are immensely grateful to him. Thanks too to Robert Geyer for his support.

A crack team from Lancaster runs all the Westminster Faith Debates (thanks to Virgin Trains on the West Coast Mainline). The Head of Staff and Chief Co-ordinator is Peta Ainsworth. Rebecca Catto worked closely with Peta, Linda and Charles, assisting us all. Norman Winter, who has helped with this book, is also responsible for audio and podcasts. Martin Seddon mans the cameras and does the video editing. Simon Reader was our ace Tweeter. Russell Reader helped with marketing, and Lisa Tremble of Lexington Communications advised on media strategy. Student interns who came down from Lancaster to help us included Sheldon Kent, Tom Moylan and Becky Joyce. Student helpers from London included Stephanie Eldridge, Shanon Mohd Sidik and Jacquelyn Strey. Thanks to you all.

The book was the brainchild of David Moloney at DLT. Thanks to him for the encouragement.

Enthusiastic audiences spurred us on and contributed many of the best questions, some reproduced here.

Finally, thanks to all the speakers, who gave their time so generously and free of charge. They set an excellent example of how to stand up for what you believe and disagree respectfully.

CHAPTER ONE
Abortion and stem cell research – does the embryo have a 'soul'?

We evolve over time from the moment of our
conception. From the very beginning, therefore, it
seems to me we are human beings and potentially
human persons.

Revd Dr Gerard Hughes

God starts life. God will end your life. This is why
suicide, assisted suicide, euthanasia, and abortion are
all prohibited in our religion.

Dr Majid Katme

If we wish to recommend legislation policy in a multi-
faith, multi-cultural or no-faith society like ours we have
to use arguments and evidence that are in principle
available and acceptable by all citizens.

Professor John Harris

Opening Comment by **CHARLES CLARKE**

This debate, about the moment at which society considers life to begin, has enormous implications for individuals, communities and governments across the world. It is also the point at which religions and faiths have their greatest impact, whether positive or negative, upon the culture and humanity of the world.

Over centuries contraception and abortion have been central issues in every society. But in recent decades rapid scientific and technological change, with the invention of the contraceptive pill and the potential of stem cell research, have pushed the issue to the very forefront of concern.

The potential power of these changes, for example in enabling societies to control more directly the speed of population change, and in permitting medical discoveries which could improve life dramatically for people who otherwise have very poor prospects, has placed religious and ethical concerns about these techniques under the spotlight.

This is reflected in the figures, published for this debate, which demonstrate that only a relatively small proportion of the adherents of the main religions follow the tenets of their religious leaders, and the proportions are lower still for the society as a whole.

The debate was not intended to judge the religious and ethical views about the moment at which life begins, but to try and clarify what they are and to explore the extent to which it might be possible to see how religious doctrine could evolve to lessen the sharp conflicts between religion and the wider society which can be so damaging.

Personally I welcomed the information that large numbers of people in no way favoured, or wanted, abortion, but nevertheless thought that others should have the legal right to make that choice.

I also very much valued the observations in the debate to the effect that the issues were less about 'pro- or anti-life' than the balancing of different pro-life values. This allows discussion to take place in a more tolerant and understanding way.

 ## Setting the scene – by **LINDA WOODHEAD**

Let me introduce this debate with some basic facts and figures about abortion and stem cell research in Britain today.

In 2011 there were 189,931 abortions among residents of England and Wales. That is 17.5 per 1,000 women, compared with 12 per 1,000 in Scotland. The number of abortions carried out in this country has been falling in recent years (Dept. of Health, Abortion Statistics, England and Wales: 2011).

At what stage of development are abortions carried out? The vast majority, 91% of abortions, are carried out under 13 weeks, and most under 10 weeks. Just 1% are carried out on the grounds of the risk that the child will be born handicapped.

What about attitudes to abortion? Our YouGov survey finds that religious attitudes are not significantly different from those of the general population (Figure 1). The majority of religious people, like the majority of non-religious people, are in favour of retaining or even raising the current 24-week limit on legal abortion (43% of religious people, 46% of the general population). A slightly higher number of religious people (9%) would like to see a ban on abortion than the general population (7%), but the numbers are small.

	Religious people	General population
Retain or raise 24-week limit	43%	46%
Lower the 24-week limit	30%	28%
Ban abortion	9%	7%

Figure 1: YouGov for Westminster Faith Debates 2013.

Our poll also shows us that, overall, anti-abortion sentiment has been declining, and support for the current abortion law has been growing. This is interesting, given that there has been a significant amount of campaigning to ban or to lower the time limit for abortion – it does not seem to have worked.

Turning to differences between religious groups, among those we surveyed, Catholics, Muslims and Baptists are most hostile to abortion – but not all Catholics, Muslims and Baptists. On the basis of our survey we can construct a profile of those who are opposed to abortion. The most important factors which predict opposition to abortion:

- believing in God with great certainty
- relying most strongly on God, scripture and religious teachings for guidance

- belonging to a religion whose leaders give a strong anti-abortion message. These are strictly religious people, or 'Godfearers'.

When do people think that human life begins (or, as some religious people would put it, that the embryo is 'ensouled')? The figures from our poll are surprisingly high. Forty-four per cent of people believe that human life begins at conception, 30% that it begins at some time during pregnancy, 17% when the baby is born, and 8% 'don't know'.

What is surprising is that, despite the fact that a lot of people believe that life begins at conception, it doesn't necessarily mean that they are anti-abortion (Figure 2).

		Current time limit should be retained or relaxed	Time Limit should be reduced	Abortion should be banned altogether
Human life begins (don't knows omitted)	**at conception** 44%	41%	43%	16%
	some time in pregnancy 30%	64%	32%	4%
	at birth 17%	81%	16%	3%

Figure 2: YouGov for Westminster Faith Debates 2013.

As for stem cell research, in this country it is legal to take cells for research use from human embryos under two weeks old. A Eurobarometer poll carried out in 2010 finds that 61% of people are in favour of this as long as it's regulated by strict laws.

How can we explain these surprising findings, and in particular the fact that many people believe that life begins at conception, but are not in favour of tightening the current law permitting abortions up to 24 weeks?

My suggestion is that the debate is not really between people who are 100% 'pro-life' (and anti-abortion) or 100% pro-choice (and pro-abortion). Hardly anyone thinks that abortions are 'good' or simply a matter of free choice – something to be treated lightly. A Comres survey carried out in May 2006 shows that many people (53%) think that the current rate of around 200,000 abortions each year is too high. Only 10% want easier access to abortion. Many (61%) agree that abortion law has not kept up with our knowledge of early development in the womb, and 67% feel that aborting a baby after six months, the legal limit, is cruel. Nevertheless, 65% agree that a woman's right to choose outweighs the right to life of the unborn.

What these findings show is that the life of the embryo is valued by many people. But most people still consider the rights of mother, siblings and others affected by a new birth to be more compelling than the rights of early embryos.

So in the debates over abortion, we are really dealing with disagreement between two different sorts of pro-life opinion, rather than simply pro-life v pro-choice. Each side of the debate means something different by 'life'. For some it is the sheer fact of 'life' beginning in a cluster of cells that counts. But for more people, what really matters is a full and fulfilled life. So it is permissible to abort an embryo if the quality of life of the mother and other family members would be seriously affected by having another child. This is not an argument between religious and secular people but between two competing understandings of life.

THE DEBATE

DAVID ALBERT JONES, Director of the Anscombe Bioethics Centre[1]

[1] Dr David Albert Jones is a Roman Catholic ethicist, and Visiting Professor at St Mary's University College in Twickenham. His books include *The Soul of the Embryo: An enquiry into the status of the human embryo in the Christian tradition* (Continuum, 2004).

I think there are a number of possible positions here on the question which I want to look at, which is 'When did I begin?' Clearly we now do exist, so at some point we went from not existing to existing. When did we begin to be? This has implications for stem cell research and for abortion. It's not the only issue in either case but it's important and something that we don't bear in mind enough.

First we must ask a key question: 'What am I?' You may say, 'What I think I am most fundamentally is a living individual, a living being, a biological living being, that's what I am. I've done different things, I've changed in different ways but I am a living individual.' So the question then is, 'When does this living human individual start?' In most cases, at fertilisation. A small percentage started as a single zygote and then they're twins. And a very tiny percentage begin as embryos which have been created in vitro by somatic cell nuclear transfer. So I think that the most credible answer for most people is 'at fertilisation', when a sperm and egg come together.

The law, for example the law about research on stem cells, says 14 days is a significant period in the life of the embryo. Fourteen days after what? What are we counting from? We are counting from fertilisation. Before that you have two things, sperm and egg, and after that you have one thing. That's why fertilisation is significant.

Pictures illustrate this point. When I got married, my mother had pictures of myself and my twin sister as babies. She thought it would be very amusing to show people and see if they could sort out which was which. These days friends of mine who have children not only have pictures of babies in their wallet but they have little pictures of ultrasound scans. So no doubt when their children get married, they will have the embarrassment of not only the pictures of them as a baby but the picture of the ultrasound. Some children are conceived as a result of fertility treatment in which you bring sperm and egg together in a petri dish. So you might have a photograph of that, and you can imagine some poor person in the future having in their wallet not only a picture of two babies lying on a blanket but also a picture of an ultrasound of two little babies and also a picture of two embryos. And they might say, 'One's a boy, one's a girl, and we're not quite sure which one's which, but there they are. And that was me as a baby and that was me in the womb and that was me as an embryo.'

That's why I think there is a continuity from fertilisation onwards of the same living individual, and why – in traditional Christian language – the embryo has a soul from that point on.

GERARD HUGHES, Jesuit priest and Tutor in Philosophy, Oxford University[2]

Suppose you bought a car and they said it would be delivered to your door. You turn up that evening expecting to see the car outside the door, and what you've got on the lawn is a heap of car parts. You ring up the dealer and say, 'I thought you were going to give me a car'. And he says, 'I'm sorry. Was there anything missing?'

The difference between a heap of car parts and a car is the way they're put together. That's the key difference. The way they're put together is not an extra part and it is not a thing at all. I think about a soul in the same way. A soul is a particular way of putting bits of a living organism together. Even if 80% of my DNA or more is indistinguishable from a tomato, I'm very distinct from a tomato because of the way my ingredients are put together and therefore function, so then I can feel, walk and love. The assembly is not a separate part, so I do not think that a soul is a thing. But I do think it's crucially important that we are put together in a very unique way.

The functions that we're capable of performing start off by being very few. I suppose most living things are quite similar in the early stage of their development. But we gradually develop. The potential which was there from the beginning, if it is not

[2] Gerard Hughes SJ teaches philosophy at the University of Oxford. His books include *Fidelity without Fundamentalism: A dialogue with tradition* (Darton, Longman & Todd, 2010) and *Is God to Blame?*, Veritas, 2007).

impeded for one reason or another, that's what produces 'us' at the end of the day. We evolve over time from the moment of our conception. From the very beginning, therefore, it seems to me we are human beings and potentially human persons. We are human beings because our DNA is human. But a human person is defined in terms of being able to perform the activities which are characteristic of a person rather than a tomato. So I think that we become persons gradually over time. The embryo is a potential person, but that is very different – and morally different – from being a person. So I want to distinguish between being human beings from the moment of conception, and being human persons.

If the crucial thing about a human person is that it can think, most of us become persons quite late on. I am not going to say when; I have no idea when babies in the womb start to think. It is something which we develop gradually. It seems to me that it is part of being a human person to raise all these critical, moral issues. The rights that things have depend on the kind of things they are, and that depends on what they can do. I think that any living thing with sentience has got some rights. I don't think fleas have got rights, but I think animals have. We have rights from that point at which we are able to be sensitive to pain, for example. But a foetus doesn't have a right to get married. You gradually pick up rights as your development continues. I don't think we can draw any sharp lines.

ABDUL MAJID KATME, spokesperson for the Islamic Medical Association of the UK[3]

The key reference point for the 1,600 million Muslims in the world is the holy book, the Qur'an, and the sayings of the final Prophet Muhammad (peace be upon him). Modern doctors have been astonished at the amount of embryological information in the

[3] Dr Abdul Majid Katme is a Muslim born in Lebanon and educated in Egypt who came to Britain in 1972 to practise psychiatry. He promotes Muslim teaching on the sanctity of life and other medical issues.

Qur'an, and how compatible it is with modern scientific knowledge. So when as Muslims we pray, we read some verses from the Qur'an and think about embryology and the creation of a child.

We visualise during our prayers the embryo/foetus and his or her wonderful development. We try to understand in a tone of admiration for the Creator, the best Designer, the Programmer, who creates human beings beautifully, wonderfully, stage by stage. The embryo/foetus is in our mind all the time: we admire the Creator and we respect and try to protect the life of every embryo or foetus.

We have a clear-cut statement in the holy Qur'an that God is the Owner of life. God starts life. God will end your life and my life. This is why suicide, assisted suicide, euthanasia and abortion are all prohibited in our religion. Sanctity of life is crucial and basic in our beliefs.

When Islam emerged 1,400 years ago there was no word for abortion. (Though it does talk of miscarriage when a woman loses her baby suddenly.) So from fertilisation, which the Qur'an calls *nutfatul amshaj* (the mixing of sperm and egg), we stop, admire, respect, remember the Creator, the best Designer and the Owner of life and think at all times about protecting this new wonderful human being.

There are seven stages in embryology according to Islam. From fertilisation we are human or potentially human but, at about six week's pregnancy, or 42 days, is a big landmark. This is when skin, muscle, bone, hearing, vision, final gender and so forth are formed, so one clear Islamic view based on Prophetic statements is that the soul is breathed in just after 42 days.

Here I must mention another popular Muslim view. Unfortunately due to some misinterpretation of a Prophetic saying, some Muslim scholars say that the soul is breathed in after 120 days from conception, four months after fertilisation. There is disagreement on this point among other scholars, who believe the soul is breathed in at about six week's pregnancy. The wrong view led some scholars to say abortion can be carried out up to four months into pregnancy – I and other scholars strongly oppose this view.

Abortion is not mentioned in the holy scriptures, and there is a very good indication that abortion did not take place in the Prophet's years. There is no line in the Qur'an or in the sayings of the final Prophet Muhammad which allows abortion at any stage in the pregnancy. But recently many Muslim scholars allowed abortion only if the life of the mother was in danger from continuation of the pregnancy. This is an Islamic ruling to save the life of the mother.

Some Muslim scholars allowed abortion before six weeks of pregnancy but only for good reasons. After six weeks it is absolutely forbidden. The foetus is a human being, and it is godly, because God breathes the soul into it about this time. Thus the pro-life ideal concept is deeply rooted in our religion and we need to inform many Muslims about its foundation in our holy scriptures. We appeal today for all Muslims to get involved in the pro-life campaign as an Islamic duty, especially since so many innocent unborn babies are killed in Britain every day through abortion.

As regards stem cell research, obviously the embryo is sacrosanct. If you are coming to make an embryo only in order to harvest cells and kill the soul of the embryo, it is wrong and we should not do it and Islam opposes it. We have a clear fatwa/ Islamic ruling against embryonic stem cell research using cells from an embryo. Islam supports stem cell research. Islam supports adult stem cell research, which has great potential for the treatment of many diseases. We believe this is the way forward, but more scientific research in the field of adult stem cells is needed.

JOHN HARRIS, Director of the Institute for Science, Ethics and Innovation at the University of Manchester[4]

[4] Professor John Harris, an atheist, is Professor of Bioethics at the University of Manchester. He has written widely on biomedical ethics and has acted as an ethical consultant to the European Parliament, the European Commission, the World Health Organisation and the UK Department of Health.

I don't have a spiritual or religious cell in my body, nor do I wish to have any of those sorts of cells. I don't have a soul, depending on how you would define a soul, and I don't think any of you do either.

To me, the question 'When did I begin?' is an uninteresting one. I may be curious about the circumstances of my procreation – like Tristram Shandy in Laurence Sterne's novel – but it's not moral curiosity. The question that matters is: when did I begin to matter morally? When did I start to have the sort of value that makes my life worth saving?

Let me mention a few facts that you may think relevant. The abnormality rate for births in the world is around 6%. Almost 8 million babies are born every year with serious birth defects of genetic or partially genetic origin. If you agree with me that this is a tragedy and it would be much better if that figure were lower or indeed zero, then a number of things follow. One is that we may wish to prevent those births; another is that we may wish to use the technologies available to us including stem cell research to prevent those sorts of things happening. That's one of the things that I think it should mean to be pro-life. For me, being pro-life means being be pro- 'lives that are more worth living'.

Secondly, a couple of puzzles for those of you – like David Jones and Majid Katme – who think life begins at fertilisation. We know that if you have an embryo in a laboratory dish at the stage where all the cells are still totipotent then you can split that cell mass, just as happens when identical twins are formed *in utero*. You can split it; you can split the early embryo into clumps which will develop. So those who think ensoulment at fertilisation is a meaningful concept have a problem over whether or not we create extra souls by doing that. And another thing that we know now from research is that you can push them all together again. One soul or many?

Then I think about embryo loss. Normal human sexual reproduction is incredibly inefficient. It has between an 80% and a 60% failure rate. If it had been invented as a reproductive technology it would never have been licensed. It's incredibly wasteful and destructive of embryos. So if you really value embryos from the moment of conception, don't have unprotected intercourse – because each of you sitting in this room is here over the dead bodies of between three and five of your siblings that were probably lost in the very first month of development unnoticed by your mothers.

So if it is legitimate to destroy embryos for the sake of future generations, then is it surely legitimate to destroy embryos for something as comparably important as creating new generations with a good quality of life. I think any rational person would think that it is as important to save existing lives, to remove misery and foreshortened lives, as it is to create new generations. Therefore if we are entitled, as we clearly believe, to kill embryos, to cause their destruction knowingly and deliberately, in order to get future generations, then it is equally justified to do so for the sake of ameliorating the lives of existing generations – as in stem cell research.

DISCUSSION

Should abortion laws be tightened?

David Albert Jones Yes. I think that both with abortion and stem cell research we have far, far more permissive laws than most other countries. I think that we disregard embryonic life, we allow experimentation on embryos and the creation of embryos for experimentation, in a way which most civilised countries do not. And I think that we don't have to have the laws that we have and I would like it if more people were as concerned about them as I am. I have no realistic expectation that that's imminent. But I think we need to try to persuade people to enact laws which support a more just system which encourages people to do the right thing and discourages them from doing things that we think are harmful.

Gerard Hughes On the whole I think the current laws are as sensible as you're going to get. And the reason why I can say that is because, with all due respect, I don't honestly think that religion ought to have a separate voice in these issues. Because religious beliefs have to interact with the best secular knowledge. The religious beliefs that Galileo challenged had to be abandoned, and quite rightly, because religion has to change as we understand our world better.

Linda Woodhead What this debate between David and Gerry clearly shows is that Catholics don't always agree! There are two very different Catholic views here, both widely shared.

John Harris I just wanted to put, I think, a similar point to Gerry in a different way. If we wish to recommend legislation policy in a multi-faith, multi-cultural or no-faith society like ours we have to use arguments and evidence that are in principle available and acceptable to all citizens. And this means we can't appeal simply to arguments that will only have weight with particular religions or particular cultures.

Disability and abortion

Alex Bishop I'm from Westminster School. I was wondering: if you had a pregnancy which you'd screened before the 12-week limit that we currently have, and you knew that that child was going to be born with a genetic disease, do you not think that your decision not to abort that pregnancy is directly contributing to that child's potential suffering for all the years that they will live with that genetic problem?

David Albert Jones I was very moved during the Paralympics to see examples of human excellence, examples of the human spirit of a wide variety of kinds, and I certainly wouldn't wish to say that just because someone had a disability they didn't therefore have a worthwhile life. I think that finding ways to improve people's quality of life is a very good thing, but saying in advance that somebody won't have a certain quality of life because they have a disability is objectionable.

Gerard Hughes There are certain handicaps with which a person can be born which obviously they would prefer not to have, but if you ask them, 'Do you wish you'd never been born?', many might say, 'No, of course I don't wish that.' So I don't think there's going to be one answer to that question. In all of these cases I think you've got to look at what this human being is, and the point at which it becomes a person and starts to have rights.

Women's rights in the abortion debate

Abby Day I'm from the University of Kent. This has been a debate between men. But as your YouGov poll showed, most people would agree that issues about abortion actually should be a choice of a woman.

Gerard Hughes It seems to me that there are one or two instances in which it's quite obvious that a woman has an interest in what is happening which are completely different from the interests that any man could have, and rape is an obvious example. So I think there's a good case for saying that a woman's interest in her future life and everything else is intimately connected with pregnancy, and so she has a unique voice. But I think there are many other issues concerning the rights of much older foetuses where it's not obvious that the woman's own life is more important than that of the baby. It may be, but I don't think it's obvious and the mere fact that I'm a woman doesn't actually say so one way rather than another. So if it is the case that a woman would see something which these four men don't see I could quite believe it but I have to be shown what that is and I don't think 'well I'm a woman so I can determine the matter,' I don't think that's a good reason. But 'I'm a woman and I can show you something that you men have missed,' might well be a good reason. You've got to have something which you can share with everybody with a bit of care and persuasion so that they can see what you're on about.

John Harris   It doesn't follow from the fact that someone is of a particular gender that they have a particular right either to speak or to have a particular conclusion. The argument about the legitimacy of abortion follows from either an argument about the relative moral status of the mother and the baby or possibly from a self-defence type argument if the baby is threatening the life of the mother. It doesn't follow simply from the fact that the person making the decision is pregnant or is a woman, though I would also agree with Gerard that that might give the woman a unique insight into the situation and might engage our compassion in all sorts of cases as well. So for me women's rights are not a premise in a moral argument; like everything else for me they are a conclusion of the moral argument.

Majid Katme   The only fatwa permitting abortion [is] if the life of the mother is definitely in danger. Not like what they do today – citing merely the mental health of the mother, which is very questionable. And this is, by the way, a man-made Islamic ruling, we don't have permission in the holy scripture to kill anyone. Yes it is important to protect the life of the mother. But I always add: please try to take this pregnant woman to hospital, monitor her, allow her to carry on the pregnancy if possible.

The natural loss of embryos

Alan Pavelin   I'd like to challenge John Harris's point of view on embryonic loss. Embryonic loss is simply a natural death, which we all experience, so aren't you saying in effect that because natural death happens to everybody, including embryos, therefore deliberate killing is justified? I can't see the logic behind that.

Elizabeth Berry   I'm a retired civil servant. My question is not so much a question to be answered but an invitation to Professor Harris to clarify what he appears to be doing which is to base a very large edifice on a very shaky foundation, namely *post hoc ergo propter hoc*. It's surely wrong to say that the inevitable deaths of embryos following intercourse is an intended action of the parties to the intercourse?

John Harris   'After something because of something.' The fallacy that if something follows something it's because of it. What I was claiming is that we are responsible not only for what we wish to produce, for the effects that we wish to produce, but also for the effects that we deliberately and knowingly produce whether we would wish them or not. So we are responsible if we perform an act, sexual reproduction, which we know will result in the deaths of embryos. If we think that that's a bad thing – as some of my colleagues do but I don't – then we are fully responsible for that. I don't think that involves the fallacy that you attributed to it.

Time limits, personhood and euthanasia

Harnee Dhaliwal   I'm a business management student at the University of Lancaster and my question is to Professor John Harris. I think at the start of the debate you clearly implied that it's better to terminate the embryos which potentially have genetic diseases. Doesn't that raise an ethical question of suicide and murder? As a parent, am I allowed to kill my, let's say, 13-year-old son or daughter just because they have suddenly got a disease or an illness? Secondly, maybe old people can use the same excuse and justify killing themselves just because they've developed an illness, and don't you think that creates a dilemma and mentality in a society that it's OK to end life just because you've got an illness?

Michaela Aston   I'm interested in the distinction that you seem to be bringing up between a human being and a person. A few months ago it hit the newspapers, suggesting that there's no difference in the moral status of the child in the womb and after birth. And I think, Professor John Harris, about ten years ago, you actually said that, and said that infanticide in certain circumstances would be fine. Now presumably this is an extension of the distinction between the value of a human being and a person. So it's not enough to be a human being any more, you have to be a 'human doing', you have to actually prove that you can be a 'person'. So my question is, isn't this idea of personhood a philosophical one which we're never going to be able to be in agreement on, and if it's going to be the basis of decisions about ending life, then an awful lot of people who can't prove they are persons aren't safe really?

John Harris   There are many distinctions that we need to make here. There is a difference between defending something and advocating it. There is a difference between defending it and saying that the arguments for or against it are inadequate. So on the question of infanticide or after-birth abortion, we currently in this country have a law which makes abortion legal right up to term, right up to birth, right up to the end of the third trimester for serious foetal handicap.

Now there is an inconsistency here which goes both ways. You have to ask what has happened in the passage down the birth canal, such that the entity is unprotected at one end and protected at the other. You have to think that there's some change that has taken place in that very short geographical space, and depending on the speed of the delivery temporal space as well, such that there is a moral difference, a difference in value at one end or the other.

I think that account is absent. I don't think anybody has

given a satisfactory account of how that could be ... All I'm pointing out is an inconsistency. What I am interested in is in our account of what it is that makes lives morally important, valuable, worth saving, wrong to take and so on, where that starts to apply to the emerging human individual.

Gerard Hughes I don't suppose anybody would want to deny that, say, a living sperm cell or a living ovum is a living, human thing. It's obviously human; it doesn't belong to any other species. Similarly, a fertilised ovum, an embryo, is obviously a living human thing and in this case – unlike them separately – is potentially a human person. When it becomes a human person is not a clear thing. It's potentially a person and if it aborts spontaneously that potential is never realised.

David Albert Jones On the personhood stuff I just think that we should be very, very suspicious of the idea that there's a distinction between persons and human beings such as you can have human non-persons. I think that the notion of non-persons is like that of non-words, it's a way of trying to eradicate a certain kind of status. I think if somebody were in a coma for six months or nine months and they had no sentience at all during that time ... I think you would say this is a person who is at the moment unconscious, but later we hope will recover, and if that can be true, nine months in a coma is as nine months in the womb.

Majid Katme I'm just wondering, watching some of my colleagues using philosophical arguments here, sometimes I feel it is necessary to be frank ... I just cannot understand how John Harris can say ... you can kill a child after birth. Where are we going today? Where is our basic humanity? If you listen, what he said ...

John Harris ... That's not what I said or have ever said, just for the record ...

30

Majid Katme ... So philosophical. I wonder now, maybe we should avoid a lot of philosophy today. There's basic human nature, basic human feeling in every one of us and it's put in our heart and soul by God Almighty. To justify in the case of a baby about to be born disabled, kill him, kill her – and now you say even after he's born. You celebrate. John said you can kill this child. I think we're going too far; please avoid a lot of philosophy.

John Harris I am sorry that nuanced argument is becoming relatively impossible, but nonetheless I guess that is the nature of public utterances. I don't think illness is a justification for ending life. What it is is a justification for not beginning a life at a time when you don't need a justification as to whether you end it or not ... In IVF in this country, if a woman is undergoing assisted reproduction and she produces four embryos, the law will only permit her to implant two. The other two can be frozen for future use, but may never be used. If she decides not to use them they may be destroyed or they may be donated to other women. Should she implant those about whom the best guess is that they will have the best of the lives that we can predict from let us say the genetic make-up of that embryo? I think she should, I think she would be wrong not to make that choice, and she can make it on the basis of disability, but only because she is entitled not to create any of those lives.

But you and me; I've got lots of problems, health and other sorts, I don't think they diminish the value of my life one jot, nor do I think my life's value is diminished by the fact that I am a lot older than you and therefore have less un-elapsed time left to me. I think you and I should be valued equally, I hope you agree.

Stem cell research

Anonymous question I was just wondering if a cell which is a non-sex cell was then engineered to become totipotent, and then has the same possible ability to form a full human being as, say, a fertilised egg cell, would then that use in treatment of medical conditions and its subsequent destruction be the same kind of destruction as that of a human being, and would it be murder of a human being as if an embryo was used?

Gerard Hughes I don't know whether anybody else in the audience is in a position to contradict me, but I really do believe that it's quite possible now from adult cells to produce stem cells which are extremely flexible. As far as I know it's not possible to produce stem cells from adult cells which thereby are exactly like embryos and can then develop.

John Harris Nobody's doing it precisely because they're worried about it being called the creation of embryos. It's certainly in principle possible and I'm pretty sure that it will prove to be possible. But if you create a totipotent cell you're effectively creating an embryo.

Gerard Hughes OK, but then you don't have to use them for that purpose.

David Albert Jones That would be a rather circuitous way to create an embryo and you would have the same kind of issues you have with embryos.

John Harris May I just come in scientifically on that? Unfortunately at the moment the only way that it is possible to tell the difference between a pluripotent cell, that is to say a cell that could become almost any part of a resulting organism but not the whole thing, and a totipotent cell, which is effectively an embryo, is retrospectively. You see what it grows into and then you know whether it was totipotent or pluripotent. When we have a way of finding that out, in advance of seeing how it develops, then we will know whether what you just said is true.

Majid Katme   Many years back I presented a Muslim view, a medical view, to the House of Lords. There was a consultation on stem cells. I read daily and I receive a lot of medical news about the high–success work with adult stem cells. Just go to the website www.stemcellresearch.org; I tend to believe lately there is a lot of cover–up about success in adult stem cell research and there are people pushing all the time for embryonic stem cells.

SOME MEDIA REACTION

The success of adult stem cell research is being underplayed in favour of more controversial work using embryonic cells, according to religious figures who blame 'aggressive secularism' and the 'personal investment' of researchers in their projects for the alleged bias.

Elizabeth Gibney, *Times Higher Education*, 21 February 2013

Anti-abortion sentiment in Britain is declining, according to a YouGov poll which also found that support for keeping or even relaxing the current 24-week limit on terminations is on the rise.

Ben Quinn, *Guardian*, 12 February 2013

Summary: WHAT HAVE WE LEARNED? by LINDA WOODHEAD

- The current law on abortion and stem cell research seems quite settled in the UK: a majority of people agree with the status quo. However, a vocal minority continue to call strenuously for a change in the law, and present their view as 'pro-life' or pro the 'sanctity of life'. New technologies continue to throw up new questions and issues.
- This debate circles around the point at which human life begins, and whether the life of the embryo has the same rights as a human person. It reveals that there are two different ways of being 'pro-life'. For the first, life begins when an egg is fertilised (Jones), or at some later but early point (42 days for Katme).

From then on this life has the same rights as a human person. For the second, life begins at some later stage of development (Harris, Hughes). Hughes differentiates between the embryo as a 'potential person' and a 'human person' – only the latter has full human rights.

● Not all religious people have the same views on abortion, not even within the same religion. This debate is a good illustration of that: Gerard Hughes is much closer to the secular thinker John Harris in this debate than he is to his fellow Catholic, David Jones (who follows the current official Catholic teaching on abortion). This illustrates our poll findings which show that in the UK most religious people agree with the current law on abortion and stem cell research, but that a minority disagree strongly.

● The 'moral minority' in Britain – 8.5% of the population – are opposed to abortion and stem cell research. Just under half of them are strictly religious people who take their authority from scripture or religious leaders, rather than relying on their own judgement like the majority of religious and non-religious people in this country.

DISCUSSION QUESTIONS

1. Do you think that the abortion of an unborn child is comparable to taking the life of someone after their birth, and if not why not?

2. How helpful is it to ask when a developing embryo becomes a human life, and does it help you in deciding whether abortion is right or wrong?

3. Gerard Hughes made a distinction between a 'human being' and a 'human person'. If you think that is helpful, what characteristics do you think it requires to be a 'human person'?

4. David Albert Jones expressed concerns based on how we regard a person in a coma for nine months. If they have full value as a human person, should an unborn child in their nine months from conception to birth have equal moral worth and protection?

5. Would you like to see different legal time limits on abortion, depending on the reasons given for requesting an abortion?

6. Do you think the use of embryos in stem cell research, if it could lead to significant medical advances, would be justified?
7. Though it may be possible to clone human beings, is it acceptable? Does every human being have the right to be born as a result of fertilisation, whether natural or artificial?

RESOURCES

View the debate at www.faithdebates.org.uk.

Read about the ethical arguments concerning abortion in the BBC Ethics Guide, www.bbc.co.uk/ethics/abortion.

For resources and arguments against abortion, see ProLife.org.uk.

For resources and arguments in favour of the availability of abortion, see www.abortionrights.org.uk, the website of Abortion Rights, a national 'pro-choice' campaign.

John Harris, *The Value of Life* (Routledge, 1985), *On Cloning* (Routledge, 2004) and *Enhancing Evolution* (Princeton University Press, 2007) all deal with issues discussed in this debate.

David Albert Jones, 'An ethical look at human-animal embryos', *Thinking Faith*, 12 May 2008, http://www.thinkingfaith.org/articles/20080512_1.htm. This short article is about the moral status of the human embryo, and the proposal to create embryos that would be part human part animal.

David Albert Jones, 'Theologians' brief: On the place of the human embryo within the Christian tradition and the theological principles for evaluating its moral status', www.bioethics.org.uk/images/user/TheologiansBrief.pdf. This document, signed by bishops and theologians from different Christian denominations, sets out Christian reasons for respecting the human embryo. It was originally a submission to a committee of the House of Lords.

Joyce Poole, 'Ethical problems arising from new reproductive techniques', in Bernard Hoose (ed.), *Christian Ethics: An introduction* (Cassel, 1998). A carefully argued introduction to the whole topic.

CHAPTER TWO
Too much sex these days – the sexualisation of society?

All through my late teens and twenties I lived a typical hack's life and smoked a lot, drank a lot, slept around and bought the whole package about free love: sex is good, it is healthy ... I bought into all of that until I discovered it was doing me no good at all.
Jenny Taylor

The connection between sex and procreation has been broken ... Once you have broken that connection between procreation and sex it leads you down a path to a place where I think sexual activity becomes another form of entertainment.
Catherine Pepinster

The sexual revolution was a rebellion against many things. Sex was a symbol. Young people no longer wanted to be told: 'No, you can't do this. No, you can't have pleasure. No, you can't have fun.' Who had the right to tell me how to live my own life?
Linda Woodhead

Opening comment by CHARLES CLARKE

This debate addressed the perception that these days sex has a far more prominent role in the public life of society than used to be the case. This fact, which was broadly accepted through the discussion, seems to me mainly a consequence of the pace of technical, social and economic change.

Two technological developments are particularly important. First, the widespread and easy availability of contraception has weakened the once dominant view that sex was principally about reproduction, with the heavy responsibilities which that implies. Over time the balance has shifted towards recreation as well. Second, the transformation of communications through the internet means that censorship (or self-censorship) of newspapers, television and other media are almost impossible to enforce, even if it were desirable. The era of the trial of *Lady Chatterley's Lover* (1960) and theatre performances being censored by the Lord Chamberlain (until 1968) is well and truly gone. Also important is the legality, in certain circumstances, of abortion and gay sex since the passing of the Abortion Act in 1967 and the Sexual Offences Act.

In my opinion this process of change has brought about many social benefits: the place of women in society has been improved; back-street abortionists are no more; gay people can live together and commit to each other without being subject to exploitation or blackmail, and freedom of thought and expression has been advanced.

That said, many deep problems remain, most focused around children and vulnerable people. These include trafficking people for sexual abuse, and the widespread availability of porn on the internet.

But the most profound result is the need to put sex back in its proper place as part of what people are, taking its place within a set of values, or essence, or soul, in which people are properly valued and respected for their whole self and not merely for the sexual elements of their body and personality.

This challenge extends to society as a whole, including the churches: how can society be strengthened so that people can genuinely take responsibility for their own lives, avoid being bullied or pressured, and see their own behaviour as contributing to the welfare of the wider community?

Setting the scene – by **LINDA WOODHEAD**

According to the survey we commissioned for this debate, most people are pretty positive about sex. Sixty-eight per cent of us agree that sex is important for a fulfilled life, and religious people are slightly more likely than are non-religious people to agree.

One of the biggest differences in attitude is by gender – men are twice as likely (40%) as women (20%) to *strongly* agree that sex is important for a fulfilled life. But a similarly high percentage of people, 66%, also think our society is too sexualised, with too high a profile being given to sex these days. And on this point most men and women agree.

What about personal sexual ethics? Do religious people have a different code of conduct? We tried to find out by asking how guilty you would feel if you did something that crossed a line into what many religions would consider forbidden territory. Figure 1 shows the results, and again there is not a great deal of difference between those who identify with a religion and those who do not, except in relation to pornography.

Would feel guilty if you	All	All religious
used pornography for sexual stimulation	26%	55%
used contraception	5%	6%
had pre-marital sex	13%	20%
had extra-marital sex	56%	64%

Figure 1: YouGov for Westminster Faith Debates 2013.

Figure 2 breaks these findings down further, showing the responses of Anglicans, Catholics and Jews – each of which is represented by our contributors to the debate which follows. Again, there is a fairly close fit with the attitudes of the general population. This shows that most religious people ignore religious leaders and the official teachings of their religion. For example, one of the most publicised of our poll findings – in newspapers across the world – was that only 9% of self-identified Catholics say they would feel guilty using contraception, with numbers not much higher even among practising Catholics.

Would feel guilty if you	All	Anglicans	Catholics	Jews
used pornography for sexual stimulation	26%	30%	30%	31%
used contraception	5%	3%	9%	9%
had pre-marital sex	13%	12%	19%	12%
had extra-marital sex	56%	60%	57%	72%

Figure 2: YouGov for Westminster Faith Debates 2013.

So who in Britain has a different sexual ethic – who differs from the majority view? Figure 3 shows that the outliers compared with the general population are – in their very different ways – those who say they have no religion on the one hand, and the Baptists, Pentecostals and Muslims on the other. The non-religious would have the least guilt about doing any of the things in Figure 2, and conservative Protestant Christians and Muslims would have the most. That's because the latter groups take a stricter, less liberal, view of sexual morality, and believe that sex should only take place within the clear limits of a married relationship.

Other surveys reinforce the impression that most people in Britain are fairly liberal in their sexual attitudes (where liberal means they believe that individuals should be free to make their own decisions about how to live their sexual lives), and that they feel that the liberalising of attitudes towards sex that has taken place since the 1960s has made people healthier and happier.[1]

[1] For example, YOUGOV February 2006.

Would feel guilty if you	All	All non-religious	Baptists	Pentacostals	Muslims
used pornography for sexual stimulation	26%	15%	69%	89%	54%
used contraception	5%	3%	7%	9%	23%
had pre-marital sex	13%	5%	50%	76%	62%
had extra-marital sex	56%	48%	69%	89%	69%

Figure 3: YouGov for Westminster Faith Debates 2013.

This doesn't mean they think that 'anything goes'. Figure 4 shows that there is a kind of scale of what we consider to be morally acceptable. Paedophilia is the most unacceptable, contraception the least.

Please indicate whether you personally believe they are morally acceptable	
Contraception	91%
Sexual relations between an unmarried man and woman	82%
Sexual relations between two people of the same sex	58%
Pornography	40%
Prostitution	34%
Married man and/or woman having an affair	13%
Polygamy	10%
Paedophilia	1%

Figure 4: Angus Reid 2013.

Some other surveys pick up on this sense that somehow society has become too sexualised. What is meant by this? One thing is that children are put under pressure to become sexual at too early an age, or simply that the pressure is too great – especially on girls. Another is that 'the media' make the situation worse, though people are now much more concerned about the internet than TV or other media. That suggests that the ready availability of internet pornography worries many. A lot of adults, particularly men, now say they access pornography regularly, but when asked in a recent survey about the impact that pornography has on their relationship, 41% of both men and women say they are 'not sure'.[2] So maybe we're not just concerned about the sexualisation of children, maybe quite a lot of adults are concerned that it is affecting their lives as well.

THE DEBATE

 JENNY TAYLOR, journalist, director of Lapido Media, Centre for Religion in World Affairs[3]

I was a very secular journalist for some years. All through my late teens and twenties I lived a typical hack's life and smoked a lot, drank a lot, slept around and bought the whole package about free love: sex is good, it's healthy. Not just that, it's actually politically good, and through it you can make a political statement about suppressed women and about your freedom as a thinker. That was very exhilarating. Germaine Greer was my hero.

I bought into all of that until I discovered it was doing me no good at all. I was very much on a downward spiral which I didn't understand. And I'm telling you this because it is actually how I became a Christian. I am a Protestant Christian, and I became a believer through the writings of St Paul which I stumbled upon

[2] The Sex Census 2012.

[3] Dr Jenny Taylor founded Lapido Media to promote 'religious literacy' – understanding among journalists and opinion formers about how religion shapes world affairs. She is the author of *A Wild Constraint: The case for chastity* (Coninuum, 2008), anexploration of sexualisation and the destruction of childhood.

about the body, and discovered that I could actually get my life together through some power not of my own.

I kept bumping into journalists or TV producers who couldn't believe that there was actually a young journalist type of woman who really did believe in the virgin birth, and who really was trying to practise sexual continence, abstinence. So I found myself, and I still find myself, being put on panels or on television programmes or interviewed by Jenny Murray. I got asked to write a book. I've never volunteered to do this, and I really want you to know that. I respond to requests to do it because I just think that it is so terribly important.

The ideological aspect of sex is something that concerns me very greatly. And I discovered in Christianity a tradition that taught me that the body is something very honourable, and very good. There's a very high view of the body in the traditional Christian thinking which I had not come across before, and it enabled me to get my life together. I would say it saved my life.

I want young girls today to know that sex does not form persons as Freud taught and as even the Church of England today teaches. It is, I believe, abstinence that forms persons. Your character becomes stronger through sexual continence. That creates stronger societies. It is the seed, the germ of civilisation.

DONNA FREITAS, author of *Sex and the Soul* [4]

I got into the business of talking about 'hook-up culture' in the United States because my students there were grappling with it. A hook-up is a brief encounter that involves some form of sexual

[4] Dr Donna Freitas writes both fiction and non-fiction, blogs, http://donnafreitas. blogspot.co.uk/ and is a Visiting Associate Professor at Hofstra University in New York. She has conducted academic research on the attitudes of college students about sex and faith, and how these interact with sexual decision-making on campus. She is author of *Sex and the Soul: Juggling sexuality, spirituality, romance and religion on America's college campuses* (Oxford University Press, USA, 2008).

intimacy, anything from kissing to sex, with the idea that you can walk away unattached. I had one class in particular that staged a revolt against hook-up culture one semester. These were students who for the most part were rather sexually active during their college years, and I was surprised to find that they wanted to take a step back from being sexually active.

So I decided to go around talking to college students all over the US, asking them about how they felt about sex on campus. One of the things that came out of that study is that hook-up culture is the norm on college campuses in the US at private, secular, public and Catholic institutions (this does not include evangelical colleges, which is another conversation). Another was just how much angst there is around hook-up culture.

Many students explained that it's not so much the hook-up that is the problem, but living in a culture of hooking-up where there is no real alternative. The situation seems to exhaust your average college student. Even students who want to be sexually active, and who are interested in getting into relationships, tend to suffer over the long term in hook-up culture.

This is a culture saturated with sex. About 80–90% of students, depending on the college, said that you have to be casual about sex. About half of those students would add, 'And I wish you didn't have to be.' Hook-up culture is often about social capital – about appearing to be a successful person, an attractive person, someone popular. One of the things that the students don't seem to ask is, 'What do I want from sex?' They don't know where their own desire is in all of this. So there's lots of pressure to have sex, lots of bravado around sex, but very little reflection on what is sex, and a lot of ambivalence about it.

CATHERINE PEPINSTER, editor of *The Tablet*[5]

[5] Catherine Pepinster has, since 2004, been editor of *The Tablet*, a weekly Catholic journal which she describes as providing a forum for 'progressive, but responsible Catholic thinking'. She is also a broadcaster and commentator on Catholic affairs.

I've been a journalist for 30 years or so. I came to journalism after university and studying social science and politics. And before I was at university I was educated by nuns.

Somebody Jenny mentioned earlier was Germaine Greer. A couple of doors down from my convent school was a bookshop where I purchased my copy of Greer's *The Female Eunuch*, which I was fascinated by. Germaine Greer herself was also educated by nuns, to whom she has paid tribute on several occasions. She's said of these nuns that they impressed her with their communal living, their contemplation and their conversation. And she went on to say, 'The one thing the nuns don't do is take sex for granted or trivialise it or turn it into a sport. The nuns wanted us to know that sex was something very powerful and that you fooled with it at your peril.'

Like Greer, my experience of nuns was of women who impressed upon us the belief that we had minds that should be nurtured, and were not just there to become wives and mothers – we had a role to play in the world. At the same time of course there were other children for whom life was not so good; when I was at school there were men like Jimmy Savile who were grooming children, and there was abuse going on in some schools, children's homes and institutions run by the Catholic Church. There is no 'golden age' – the sexualisation of young people has gone on for years.

However, one of the things that has changed in our time and really concerns me is the extent to which young people are now sexualised not just by people that they encounter but by what goes on in their own homes via all kinds of media. That is the most tremendous change. Young people now have access to pornography, for example. We are talking about what is on your smartphone, what you are gaining access to all the time.

One thing I think is really peculiar about the time in which we live is that we are both puritanical and incredibly easy-going. We are quite easy-going about their early sexual experience, and we're allowing them to be sexualised. But we are also so careful about children that we do not let them walk down the street to go to school. When kids now think about going to university they take their parents with them to open days – something that never used to happen. So we're both very protective and infantilising of young people but at the same time we are happy for them to be sexualised from such a young age and reticent to interfere. And I'm very puzzled by that strange conundrum.

MAUREEN KENDLER, Head of Educational Programming at the London School for Jewish Studies[6]

I'm speaking tonight in quite a personal capacity, very much with the ears of a parent with four young adult children.

'Too much sex these days' and 'the sexualisation of society', I think, are two quite separate issues. I think there's the same amount of sex as there's always been. We just talk about it more and in a very different way and I really echo a great deal of what Catherine just said.

I think that the sexualisation of society is something different, and that here we somehow feel very puzzled and also quite helpless. We're sort of swept along in an unstoppable tide of sexuality, which is a negative thing. I think we're all asking how that happened and in whose interest it is. Lots of us do not like it but we are not quite sure what to do about it. And I think there is a perception that everybody, all young people, are having sex at all times, and I would love to know how Donna's US findings are replicated in the UK. My hunch, and this is really anecdotal and really unscientific, is that it's not quite as extreme as that.

Now maybe I am being naive because my children were unaccountably unwilling to have the detailed conversation with me about this topic that I wanted to have! But at least we were able to have the conversation about not having that conversation

---

[6] Maureen Kendler teaches at the London School for Jewish Studies where she is also Head of Educational Programming. She writes extensively for the Jewish press, and speaks from the perspective of Orthodox Judaism in Britain.

– something I would never have been able to do with my parents and much less them with my grandparents. And I think that is a progressive change in the sexualisation of society if you like. When my grandmother was pregnant with her second child my mother was never told. Nor was she ever remotely told anything about the facts of life, and lived in total ignorance, and I cannot think that that's a good thing.

Does every young person really feel the need to replicate the hook-up culture that they see in their beloved TV programmes in this country, such as *Fresh Meat* and *Skins*, where everybody has mostly meaningless and at best very occasionally meaningful sex? I don't really think so. Much more worrying for me is the culture of girls, and I think increasingly boys, being objectified as sexual beings, of being body obsessed, of the effect of pornography which makes ordinary young people measure themselves against these images of air-brushed perfection, inevitably feeling very undesirable and inadequate as a result. That to me is entirely pernicious.

My perspective comes from being Jewish where I hope a middle ground is sought between these two extremes: a fear of sexuality at one extreme and a culture where sex is entirely devalued at the other. We have a problem that religion is often therefore seen as anti-sex, and in Judaism really it is not. It is all for sex but very much in a context of boundaries, and that bounded context for Judaism is marriage. Sexual abstinence is absolutely not a Jewish aspiration for anyone. Judaism holds as an essential principle that people are not meant to be alone, so sex is I think part of that. It's seen as a gift to be celebrated, but one to be unwrapped at home.

But Judaism has had to acknowledge that society has changed. Premarital sex exists. Gay relationships exist. I like to think that the rabbinic community in Jewish leadership is struggling with this, not necessarily promoting or approving of those things, but that the ethical principles which govern marital relationships would still apply entirely to those relationships.

So do I want a sexualised society in which everything and

everyone is seen through a sexual lens? Absolutely not. Do I want the clock turned back to a time when sex was never spoken about, where gay people were terrified to express themselves, with all issues back in the closets? No I do not. I hope Jewish teaching can offer a middle path which might be helpful in achieving a balanced approach.

DISCUSSION

What's caused the change?

Charkes Clarke What gave rise to the change you have all identified? Is it about the media, technological changes, other aspects of culture? I think a set of interesting questions has been raised about boundaries. What do we mean by commitment, what are the boundaries of what is ethically acceptable, or acceptable within particular religious frameworks? Why has this changed, is it desirable that it has changed, can you somehow put the genie back in the bottle?

Jenny Taylor Maureen said that she felt there was always as much sex being had and done as there is now. In fact that's just not the case. Both my parents were virgins when they got married. That was actually the norm. But ten years ago one survey showed only 1% of women were still virgin when they married. That is a massive change. Another survey showed that the happiest people are the never-married women of all categories. Now, is there a correlation there [audience laughter]?

Donna Freitas We perhaps talk more about sex, but not enough in the right ways. I think it is important for high school students, and ideally their parents too, even if this embarrasses them to death, to have a conversation about what they want from sex before they go to college and what they might expect when they get there … I wonder if we need to broaden our sense of what is included under the umbrella of sex to include things like holding hands and dating, and all sorts of things that I know that a lot of college students in the US feel are not options.

Catherine Pepinster I don't think that one can put the genie back in the bottle on certain issues. Clearly the major thing that has happened in the last 50 or 60 years is that the connection between sex and procreation has been broken. Now, many people would say that that is a good thing and that they wouldn't want to see women having so many children that their health is broken. But once you have broken that connection between procreation and sex it leads you down a path to a place where I think sexual activity becomes another form of entertainment … The vast majority of people would have the view in our society that the most important thing in life is to be fulfilled. The situation we have reached is that hook-up culture, for example, is not even an issue of personal fulfilment, it is not really providing people even with that.

Maureen Kendler I think we have to ask in whose interest this hook-up culture is. I think the important thing is not so much to put the genie back in the bottle but to educate children again; it is this boundaries business, that they are not helpless. There's a whole culture of decision-making that young people, especially if they leave home, are going to be making, and I think the problem is the image of these completely helpless young adults who are unable to control their own destinies such are the forces that are against them.

Jenny Taylor Actually, parents are abetting their children in sexualisation. I met a clergywoman whose mother had actually said to her that if you do not have sex you will never get a husband … What I want to do in this conversation is to recognise the trouble that this culture is in, and recover the seriousness of what is at stake, and recover the language with which to describe it.

Linda Woodhead   An obvious answer to Charles's question about the origins of the change we are talking about is that the sexual revolution of the 1960s was a major turning point. Many people in the counter-culture of that time hoped for a society of complete love and openness, which is a fantastic ideal in many ways. 'Free love', more open sexual relations, was part of this whole package. Parents and clergy were no longer seen as arbiters of what people should or should not do, guardians of respectability. The symbols of oppression were parents and the church, and sex was the key element of repression. Women as much as men embraced the change – it is for me to decide what to do with my body and how to live my life. The pill may have made it physically possible, but a utopian dream of a free and equal society made it culturally possible.

Abby Day   I'm from the University of Kent. Just to pick up on a point made earlier on gender, I'd like to hear a little more about that. I think it hasn't been discussed how the consequences of sexualisation are different for men or for women. And certainly perhaps more dangerous for women in reifying certain stereotypes of what it is to be female. I wonder if the panellists could comment on that, particularly in the light of the idea that perhaps this sexualisation of society is not so much a product of feminism but rather a backlash against it and a reassertion of some form of patriarchal control.

Catholics and contraception

Bernard Silverman   I am a statistician, and I have helped to analyse the YouGov survey Linda spoke about. I'd like to go back to some of the questions that were asked about what people would feel guilty about. We found that 9% of Catholics would feel guilty about using contraception. So it may be that even fewer than 9% would actually not use contraception. I don't want to point a finger at the Roman Catholic Church, but we very much listen to people nowadays who are authentic. Are we in trouble because instead of hearing the rather interesting nuanced things that have been said by our four panellists what we actually hear are religious messages which are clearly not authentic?

Catherine Pepinster I guess I ought to address the issue about the Catholic Church, being the Catholic on the panel, having this dissonance between church teaching and what people actually do. I don't want to get into the technicalities of it that much, but the Catholic Church is not opposed to birth control. It has an issue with artificial birth control.

When it comes to voices of authenticity I agree we ought to ask who has got the authentic voice. Is the authentic voice coming from leaders who have a teaching which people are struggling with or ignoring, or is the authentic voice the voice of the people? Having said that, I'm now going to in a way contradict myself. The issue with contraception in the Catholic Church goes back to the document of 1968 called *Humanae Vitae*, which is well worth a read. It's not a document that involves a finger-wagging Pope laying down the law about use of the pill. It is in many ways about the human body and about love, and I don't think in talking about sex this evening we have actually mentioned the word love.

Freud, religion and sex

Nick Spencer I'm Research Director at Theos, the religion and society think tank. Everybody has been extremely sane. Everyone I think is in agreement that sex is a wonderful thing but societies have become over-sexualised and there is a profound need to re-embed sexual activity in relationships, in love, within boundaries and so on and so forth. If that had been in the public mind for the last 40 years we would not find ourselves here having this debate. What are the kind of ideological, principal drivers that have changed our sexual culture in the way it has changed over the last two generations?

Jenny Taylor   I want to thank you because I think you are trying to sound the note of alarm that I am trying to sound as well. I agree with you that we have all been rather too reasonable and we're talking about massive ideological and chemical forces … It goes back to Freud and he really did set religion against sex. He said that it was only the weaklings who colluded in the delusion of religion. Only the weaklings colluded by not having sex, by trying to justify constraints and restraints.

I would say it's not that religion is anti-sex, but just that the Christian religion has such a high view of sex and the body and understands the need for protection. Jesus himself said, 'The spirit gives life.' The body counts for nothing in terms of real fulfilment. And we have turned that absolutely on its head.

Freud wrote a book called *Civilisation and Its Discontents*. He reckoned that sexual abstinence caused mental illness. For him the only true fulfilment is recovering our animal nature. We may think we are made in the image of God as Christians, Freud really did write that we are made in the image of dog. He wrote about the way dogs have sex and that is apparently what we really, really want. I couldn't believe what I was reading when I researched for my book. All this garbage is what we have taken as gospel truth as what is good for us.

Sex, health and personal boundaries

Matthew Huish   I am a Master's student at Heythrop College doing pastoral theology. I have a particular interest in sexuality after the sexual revolution of the 1960s and basically my question relates to sexual health. Are we also discussing emotional health? My fear is that sexual health is only seen from the point of view of sexually transmitted infections. There is a space for talking about relationships, health in terms of the psycho-neurological. How can education in schools address this issue of sexualisation?

Donna Freitas   I've spent a lot of time thinking about that when

I go to colleges and universities. I often get a question about whether students who are participating in hook-up culture are scared about sexually transmitted infections and pregnancy. What they are really worried about is the fact that they don't like the pressure of hook-up culture and they didn't know how to get out of it. So one of the things that I've thought a lot about is that, at least in the United States, we'll talk about relationships as important but generally we are mostly concerned with educating around disease and infection and then rape – which is very important, don't get me wrong. But if we only educate in this area, then we're reinforcing the idea that sex is dangerous, you could get a disease or perhaps you'll be assaulted.

One of the things that's missing from hook-up culture is communication. If you communicate, you might start to like the person, which then gives complications. So you learn not to communicate around sex, which is a disaster for sexual health. And so one of the best things I think you can do to promote sexual health is talk to young people about what you do when you feel like you like someone … It's amazing how few students have ever had someone talk to them about how to ask someone out, and they don't know how to do it.

Katy I'm a student at SOAS. In the course of any of your conversations with students did you ever find that young people who held religious beliefs were more likely to understand and exercise their rights to boundaries over and above other young people?

Donna Freitas The title for my study was *Sex and the Soul*. I was originally looking to see if there was a relationship between sex and faith tradition or interest in spirituality among college students, and then came up with a whole conversation about hook-up culture. Whether or not someone's faith tradition will affect their boundaries around sex will really depend on how they practise their faith. So if they were, say, nominally Catholic, they would just laugh at the question, so there was a complete separation. But if you had students who were incredibly invested in their faith tradition so it was at the centre of their lives, and I would say the biggest block of students I could name for this would be the evangelical students that I interviewed; they could not think about sex without thinking about faith. Their lives were all about boundaries. How can I live the boundaries that are expected of me? And for some of those students it was incredibly empowering to have those boundaries, for some students it was incredibly crippling.

Is it really so bad?

Martina Krajnakova I'm from SOAS. I would like to ask if there are some ideas about the possibility that this over-sexualisation could be just a part of the evolution that we're a part of. I think that the context of our age is important because everything is so open and exposed. We might get this feeling that we're over-traumatised, and we don't really know how traumatised the previous generation felt, but because our ideas and feelings are so much more exposed that may be the problem. I'm not saying the problem is not serious, but some of us might feel that it's exaggerated.

Belinda Perrimen You said at the beginning we'd make a comparison between the US and the UK. My son's just got married at 24 after knowing someone for six years. My daughter's 20, and she's had the same boyfriend for three years. They're not unusual at university. So I guess there is a difference. They say they're reacting against the 30-year-olds who they see have messed around for so long they have no idea how to commit.

SOME MEDIA REACTION

'"Catholic guilt" is a myth – but puritanism is alive and well, says study.' Only one in 10 regular mass-going Roman Catholics in Britain feel any guilt about using contraception despite Pope Benedict's strong opposition to it, the study found. They are also much less likely to feel guilty about committing adultery, having sex before marriage or using pornography than people from many other religious groups.

John Bingham, *Daily Telegraph*, 27 February 2013

Speaking to the Huffington Post UK, Professor Woodhead said '... It shows that the official positions of churches are significantly more conservative than the members of those churches. It's interesting because secular people usually think that religious people have very conservative views on society and it's simply not true.'

Felicity A. Morse, *Huffington Post*, 26 February 2013

Summary: **WHAT HAVE WE LEARNED?** by **LINDA WOODHEAD**

- No one can say for sure whether people have more sex these days than they did in the past – we simply don't have the evidence. It's certainly true than sex outside of marriage was more frowned upon in the past, but that did not necessarily stop people doing it.
- There is, however, widespread agreement that our society has become more sexualised, meaning that sex has a higher profile. One thing this means is that sex is more often represented in the media, including the internet – in that sense, it is all around us and sexual images are hard to escape from.
- Another thing it means is that sex has a greater legitimacy – it is seen as an essential part of a 'normal' life. As a result, people are more likely to feel under pressure to present themselves as sexually desirable and sexually successful. They may feel something is wrong with them if they are not having sex or in a sexual relationship.
- On the whole, our panellists felt these were not positive developments. They were all concerned about the sexualisation of children and young people. But they disagreed about how important sex is for human fulfilment. At one end of the spectrum, Maureen Kendler echoes the Jewish view that sex and family are good for everyone. At

the other end, Jenny Taylor mourns the fact that our society allows no space for people who do not want to be in a sexual relationship – despite the fact that Christianity has traditionally celebrated celibacy (in imitation of Christ, and in order to dedicate yourself wholly to God and to other people – a model which is still followed by nuns, monks, and the clergy of the Catholic Church).

- Some of the audience felt that there was a bit too much doom and gloom in the panel discussion. Isn't sex something to enjoy and not get too hung up about, and shouldn't we celebrate the fact that we are more liberal about sexuality these days? Isn't it good that people are no longer stigmatised for their sexual choices, unless those choices harm others, particularly children? Our survey showed that most religious people share a liberal view about sexual matters with non-religious people, and that there's a good deal of consensus in society around these issues.

- The final area of discussion is around what has caused the sexualisation of society. As well as medical changes like the invention of effective means of contraception, the profound social shifts of the 1960s and since which are sometimes referred to as the 'sexual revolution' were invoked. Since the baby-boom generation (born between 1946 and 1964), each generation has tended to be more sexually liberal than the one before. In part this reflects a growing acceptance of liberal values (that each person is free to make their own life decisions), and in part a belief in equality and non-discrimination (people should not be discriminated against because of their sexuality or their gender). But it is also to do with the decline in power of the church and other 'moral guardians' of society, and a profound shift in authority. This has gone hand in hand with a deregulation of the media, which has seen the effective end of censorship, and the rise of an internet on which you can post and search for almost anything.

- It is hard to see how these changes could be reversed, even if we wanted to. If the genie is out of the bottle and people now have much more freedom about their sexual lives and are under more pressure to sexualise, that means they also have a heavier weight of personal responsibility. That must mean that socialisation and education need to equip people with the tools and the confidence to see the range of choices they have, and not be pressured into doing things they later regret.

DISCUSSION QUESTIONS

1. Do you agree with the concern expressed in the title of this event: 'Too much sex these days'?
2. Religion and family used to be important voices about what was acceptable when it came to sex, but our YouGov survey showed a wide gap between tradition and people's attitudes. Are religion and family any longer where one can go for 'authentic' guidance?
3. In a society saturated in media and commercial interests of various kinds, which cannot be trusted to have everyone's best interests at heart, which voices can young people turn to to tell the truth about sex?
4. Donna Freitas found that many US college students felt frightened by 'hook-up culture'. Is there really anything to be feared, either for the individual or for society, about sex without strings attached?
5. Catherine Pepinster talked about the way sex has become detached from procreation. Do you agree this is a fundamental shift, and is it a good thing?
6. There are differing attitudes to sex and relationships between cultures. Has the West swung so far in emphasising the freedom and rights of the individual that we have become more vulnerable to the destructive aspects of sex?

RESOURES

View the debate at www.faithdebates.org.uk.

For background on Christian ethics and an account of Catholic natural law teaching, go to *The Tablet*'s Student Zone: http://student.thetablet.co.uk/indexstudent.

For some stories of celibate life today, read http://www.bbc.co.uk/news/magazine-21739640.

Read the BBC Ethics guide regarding sexual abstinence at http://www.bbc.co.uk/ethics/contraception/abstinence_1.shtml.

'The Silver Ring Thing' is an American youth ministry which promotes a message of purity and abstinence until marriage: http://www.silverringthing.com/.

For basic information about Jewish attitudes to sexuality, see http://www.myjewishlearning.com/life/Sex_and_Sexuality/Jewish_Approaches.shtml?p=2 and http://judaism.about.com/od/sexinjudaism/a/sex.htm – which also gives perspectives from the different denominations within Judaism.

To read *Humanae Vitae*, Pope Paul VI's controversial encyclical (teaching document) on birth control, go to: http://www.vatican.va/holy_father/paul_vi/encyclicals/documents/hf_p-vi_enc_25071968_humanae-vitae_en.html.

Elizabeth Abbott, *A History of Celibacy* (Lutterworth Press, 2001) is a useful guide to the tradition of celibacy.

Shmuley Boteach, *Kosher Sex: A recipe for passion and intimacy* (Three Rivers Press, 1998) is a controversial book which defends strictly Orthodox Jewish laws of sex, often regarded as outmoded, as bringing long-term happiness and sustained passion.

Donna Freitas, *Sex and the Soul* (Oxford University Press, 2008) looks at sex and religion on American college campuses.

Jenny Taylor, *A Wild Constraint: The case for chastity* (Continuum, 2009) by the speaker, does what it says!

Andrew Yip and Sarah-Jane Page, *Religious and Sexual Identities* (Ashgate, 2013) compares experiences of young adults from different religions.

CHAPTER THREE

Is it right for religions to treat men and women differently?

I'm a woman and I don't deny that I am different from a man. But our brains aren't different and our hearts aren't different and our souls aren't different. In every respect that pertains to religion we're exactly the same. So how can it possibly be right for religions to treat us differently and particularly to treat us worse than men?

Mary Ann Sieghart

It's not politically correct at all to admit it, but I think it's true to say that most of us experience differences in the way that men and women perceive themselves and the world. It's not good or bad, but a reality that I think we deny at our peril.

Rabbi Dr Harvey Belovski

I want to emphasise that in Islam, repeated in the Qur'an many times, men and women are equal ... Where Islamic law treats men and women differently it is in the places where it takes into account their real differences, their biological differences, our psychological differences.

Fatima Barkatulla

Opening comment by **CHARLES CLARKE**

Of all the debates, this one comes nearest the heart of the current dysfunctional relationship between churches and the wider society.

The immense power of the moral and spiritual messages of the churches in Britain is fatally undermined, even destroyed, by the unwillingness of many churches to recognise the equality of women which, as society has now moved on so far, becomes almost a gratuitous insult to millions of people.

A powerful illustration is the immediate and widespread response of dismay to the Church of England's recent decision not to proceed with permitting women to become bishops. However, this particular decision is not isolated or limited to the Church of England.

As was articulated in the debate, a number of defences are offered for this discrimination. Some are legalistic, some are patronising – along the lines that women are well suited to some roles but not others – others claim biblical authority which in my view turns out to be at best uncertain, at worst fraudulent.

Whatever one thinks about their merits, these arguments do nothing to persuade most women (and also many men) that the church meets their needs or indeed the needs of wider society. As a result women leave the church or despair in their membership of it.

The polling conducted in parallel to this debate showed that, with the partial exception of Muslims and Baptists, the church leaderships and hierarchy do not speak for their membership but are in fact dangerously out of touch, tending to defend a position which is increasingly rapidly being washed away.

The churches need to be persuaded to move in line with the population as a whole, as well as their own memberships, and recognise that men and women need to be given equal treatment, as well as respect. If they fail to do this their other important messages will not be heard, their influence in society will continue to decline, and they will have fewer adherents.

It really is a message that the churches cannot afford to ignore.

Setting the scene – by **LINDA WOODHEAD**

Part of the background to this debate is the recent vote by the General Synod (decision-making body) of the Church of

England *not* to allow women to become bishops. Women can currently be ordained as priests within the Church of England, but not as bishops. In the Roman Catholic Church they cannot be ordained at all – only men can be priests and bishops and Pope. This is one example of how men and women may be treated differently within religion.

The survey we commissioned to support the debate asked people whether they approved of the Church of England's current policies towards women. Only 8% of the general population approve. Support is also low among those who identify themselves as Church of England or Anglican – only 11% approve of their own church's policy. Among those who are active churchgoers the figure rises slightly to 16%. It is lowest of all among those who say they have no religion – only 3% approve. In fact, the people who most approve of the Church of England's policies on women are Muslims – just over a quarter approve.

Support for the Roman Catholic Church's even stricter policies towards women is even lower among the general population at 6%. But Catholics are somewhat more approving – 22% of those who self-identify as Catholic approve and 31% of practising Catholics.

Would religions be better if women held senior positions? The vast majority of people in Britain think so, and that is true of religious as well as non-religious people. The differences in attitude between religious groups are not great – Hindus are the most positive about women's leadership (only 2% are not), and Muslims the least. But even among Muslims the majority are in favour of women's leadership, with only 18% against.

So who makes up the minority that is against women's leadership, the 5% of the population who think religions would be worse off if they had women leaders? Gender is an important factor – twice as many men as women hold these views – and so is the sort of guidance you rely upon in living your life. If you rely more on God, religious leaders and teachings than you do on your own judgement, then you are much more likely to disapprove of women leaders in religion.

The issue of gender difference and religion also raises the issue of God's gender. How do people think about the Supreme Being(s) – as male, female, both or neither? A survey carried out by Populus in 2008 (Figure 1) shows that most people still think of God as male. Theologians and church leaders will often say that God doesn't have gender, God is above gender. But in practice, as I know from my own research, people in Britain tend automatically to think of God in male terms – though that is more true of some religions than others. And of course there are also some old and newer religions – like Hinduism and neo-paganism – which worship female deities or a supreme Goddess. It's interesting to think about the difference this can make.

Populus (May 2008)	All	Christian	None
When you last thought about the concept of God, did you consider God as ...			
Male	62	73	48
Neither male nor female	18	15	18
Both male and female	3	4	2
Female	1	1	0
None of the above	16	7	32

Figure 1: God's gender.

THE DEBATE

ROD THOMAS, Anglican clergyman, Synod member, and Chairman of Reform[1]

[1] Rod Thomas is the Chairman of Reform, an evangelical network within the Church of England which is 'committed to upholding the Church's foundations in scripture, Creed and tradition' and which believes in 'the unique value of women's ministry in the local congregation but also in the divine order of male headship, which makes the headship of women as priests in charge, incumbents, dignitaries and bishops inappropriate'. He is vicar of St Matthew's Elburton, Plymouth, and a member of General Synod.

Some of the coverage that was given to the controversy over whether or not the Church of England should have women as bishops completely misrepresented what the debate was about. It wasn't about whether or not we should have women bishops. It was about whether and how we should make provision for those who disagree and do not want women bishops in the church.

I believe that men and women are equal before God and equally made in God's image. In that, there is no difference. And that leads me therefore to oppose discrimination in every walk of life. It's right for Christians to question things like gender stereotyping, it's right to seek to ensure equality of opportunity in terms of public policy and equal pay, and it's also right to try to overcome historic discrimination against women through encouraging positive action.

I consider that to be a Christian position and one that's common among Christians. However, I also want to say that my understanding of what the Bible teaches is that not only is there equality between men and women but there is also complementarity. In other words, there are also differences between men and women that are reflected in the different roles they have both in the family at home and the family of the church.

That position can be described in terms of support for 'male headship'. I think that's quite an emotive expression and one that it would probably be far better if I avoided completely because I think that it may suggest dominance and oppression, and lead some people to think that you're even justifying activity that could lead to abuse of women. The biblical model which I would want to stick to – the model for the home – is given predominantly in Paul's letter to the Ephesians, chapter 5.

That does indeed talk about wives submitting to husbands. However, it says much more to husbands. It says that they should be loving, that their behaviour should be self-sacrificing because they're to model their behaviour on that of Christ, and that in all of their actions they should be devoted to opening up rather than closing down options for both their wives and their family.

The model that I see in Paul's writings is of a husband occupying a role as a self-sacrificing leader so that everybody is able to get a clearer idea of what Christ is like. Similarly, the wife models discipleship so that both she and her husband are able to learn together more clearly what being a disciple of Christ involves.

What is true of family life should be true within the church. There should be differentiation of roles. And it shouldn't be about power, it should be about self-sacrificing service without power and oppression coming into it. In so far as this has been the case in the past, there is no biblical justification for such behaviour.

I've talked a lot about the Bible and some people I know would classify me and people who think like me as fundamentalists with no real place in the Church of England. I would simply want to reply that the church's doctrine is encapsulated in its canons, and Canon A5 says that the church's doctrine is 'grounded in the Holy Scriptures and in such teachings of the ancient fathers as are agreeable to the said scriptures'. To ground my position on what I understand the Bible to be saying is, I think, profoundly Anglican.

MARY ANN SIEGHART, Journalist and former assistant editor of *The Times*[2]

I will start with the blindingly obvious. I'm a woman and I don't deny that I am different from a man. But our brains aren't different and our hearts aren't different and our souls aren't different. In every respect that pertains to religion we're exactly the same. So how can it possibly be right for religions to treat us differently – and particularly to treat us worse – than men?

I was baptised and confirmed a Roman Catholic but my mother is Anglican and often took us to an Anglican church,

---

[2] Mary Ann Sieghart has spent most of her life as a journalist and broadcaster, working for *The Times*, the *Independent, The Economist*, the *Financial Times* and the BBC. She is chair of the Social Market Foundation and sits on the boards of Henderson Smaller Companies Investment Trust and DLN Digital, and on the Council of Tate Modern.

and so as I grew up I reckoned I had a choice about which to follow. I looked at what the Catholic Church was telling me, that I couldn't have any sort of leadership role, that I couldn't choose how many children to bear, that I couldn't have an abortion even if I was raped, or ask my partner to use a condom if he was HIV positive, and I thought – well, that's a pretty easy decision to make. And as I recently watched a group of elderly men decide on which elderly man was to become Pope with not a single woman having a say, and of course a woman not being allowed to become Pope herself, I felt at least partly vindicated.

But of course the Church of England is hardly free from fault, thanks to Rod Thomas and the General Synod. Like many women I felt personally insulted by the vote against women bishops. I wondered, are we somehow tainted, inferior, unloved by God? Well, of course not, so why would a religion which purports to value all humans equally in the sight of God go out of its way to alienate half of them?

And it's not just the Church of England. Almost every faith preaches some version of the golden rule and then fails to stick to it. In Christianity it's 'do unto others as you would have them do unto you'. In Buddhism: 'hurt not others in ways that you yourself would find hurtful.' For Hindus: 'one should never do that to another which one regards as injurious to one's own self.' And Muhammad taught 'as you would have people do to you do to them, and what you dislike to be done to you don't do to them.'

Yet most religions put women in positions of inferiority that men would hate. Men ought to ask themselves how they would feel if it were the other way round. How would they like their genitals being mutilated, being forcibly draped in black with only their eyes visible, or told that they couldn't drive a car, or couldn't conduct a religious service or hold positions of leadership in their religion. Now, my view is that any religion that treats women less well than men, or indeed men less well than women, is breaking the golden rule. It's morally wrong. I'm only talking about imposition here. Of course women should be free to cover their heads if that's what they prefer, or to wear a full *niqab* [face veil] because they feel that in some way it liberates them.

At least in the western world, most people have come to believe quite passionately that discriminating against people for reasons that they can't control, like the colour of their skin or their gender, is morally wrong. And that means many religions now look morally inferior to the rest of society. And religion is supposed to take a moral lead to set moral standards about the best way to behave, but instead most of them are lagging. Indeed if they didn't have special exemptions from laws they'd actually be behaving not just immorally but illegally too.

'Women and girls have been discriminated against for too long in a twisted interpretation of the word of God.' Not my words, those of Jimmy Carter, former US President who we all know is a devout Southern Baptist but has now left his church after 60 years because he couldn't bear its teachings about the so-called inferiority of women. He points out that women often served as leaders in the early Christian church but says that after the fourth century men 'twisted and distorted Holy Scriptures to perpetuate their ascendant positions within the religious hierarchy. The truth is that male religious leaders have had and still have an option to interpret holy teachings either to exult or subjugate women. They have for their own selfish ends overwhelmingly chosen the latter.'

He's right. It's selfishness, the determination of men to hold on to a better position at the expense of women, that has allowed continued discrimination against women in almost all religions. Which is odd, isn't it, because the sin that the golden rule which they all agree on was designed to thwart is selfishness: don't put yourself first but do as you would be done by.

HARVEY BELOVSKI, Jewish rabbi of the Orthodox Golders Green Synagogue[3]

I'm speaking not just as rabbi but as a husband, a rabbinical organisational consultant, an adviser to communities, and the father of four very lovely and pretty feisty daughters. I'm a passionate believer in empowering men and women in all aspects of their lives, particularly their spiritual lives … But I also want to live in a society where religious life and the opportunities it provides discourage all spurious distinctions, particularly gender distinctions, but responds properly to differences that are real.

I'd been quite cynical in the past about gender distinctions and we can argue probably well beyond this debate as to whether they are germane to religious life. My wife and I have boy–girl twins. Boys and girls do respond to similar experiences in rather different ways. The debate goes on as to whether boys and girls, men and women, are hard-wired differently. It's not politically correct to admit it, but I think it's true to say that most of us experience differences in the way that men and women perceive themselves and the world. It's not good or bad, but a reality that I think we deny at our peril, and one that I believe our religious life and teaching should respond to.

It's well known that Jewish religious life focuses mostly on the home and on teaching. In those areas men and women have equal roles. They can be teachers, leaders in every respect, because this is where values, traditions, practices are discussed, transmitted and experienced for the next generation.

It's true that in certain areas of Jewish life men and women have different public roles. They both have senior roles both in teaching and other areas of life, but it's true that in public ritual there are obvious gender disparities. In Orthodox synagogues

[3] Rabbi Harvey Belovski has been rabbi of the Golders Green congregation since 2003. He combines this with a wide range of other roles in the Jewish community in London, further afield and online. He specialises in the teaching and interpretation of the Torah, the Jewish scriptures. He researches and teaches at the London School for Jewish Studies, writes a blog, http://www.rabbibelovski.co.uk/, and is a relationship counsellor. He and his wife Vicki have seven children.

many areas of public ritual are not led by women, and rabbis are men. It's important to clarify a particularly Jewish stance on ritual and ritual life and a place of worship. It's not just about performing a set of rituals, in which case it would be unthinkable that men and women or in fact any groups had different opportunities. It's about sensing the magnificent presence of God, celebrating self, building society, and understanding the ways of God through prayer and the Jewish scriptures.

I'm proud to be constantly rethinking these boundaries. I'm also perfectly happy to admit that some of them are historic. Some of them are based on particular historical contexts, and as a responsible religious leader I'm very deeply aware of the dissonance between modernity and tradition. I lead my colleagues in rethinking these boundaries and recognising that we need to constantly re-evaluate the difference between those gender distinctions that are real and those that are tinged with misogyny of the past, and be responsive to actual distinctions. If we're not alert as religious leaders to unexplained gender distinctions, we risk appearing alienating and insensitive. I want to try to build a religious life that responds to rather than ignores the nuanced spiritual needs of both women and men.

FATIMA BARKATULLA, Islamic scholar, lecturer, writer and broadcaster[4]

I think we need to be clear on what we mean by 'religion' and what we mean by 'differently'. What is it to treat something the same, and what is it to treat something equally?

Imagine that you're a parent and you're taking your children to the shoe shop. In an attempt to treat them equally you say to them, 'I'm going to get you exactly the same shoes,

[4] Fatima Barkatulla is a British-born Muslim who has pursued Islamic studies both in Britain and the Middle East, especially Egypt. She teaches for IERA, the Islamic Education and Research Academy, and writes for a range of Muslim publications as well as mainstream print and broadcast media. She combines this with family life with her husband and 'four energetic children'.

exactly the same size, exactly the same type, regardless of what your individual needs are, regardless of the differences between you, and that's what I consider to be equality.' That is actually not equality, but sameness. You're trying to treat each of your children in the same way, but it's a simplistic way of treating them. Equality would be making sure they have the same quality of shoes, for example, but taking into account their differences – different shoe sizes, preferences and so on. So when we talk about difference, *distinguishing between* things is not necessarily *discriminating against* things.

Also, what is 'religion'? As a Muslim, religion to me is the guidance, the laws, the way of life, revealed by God our Creator for human beings through messengers in revelation. So when you're asking me the question, 'Is it right for religions to treat men and women differently?' you're really asking 'Is it right for God to treat men and women differently?' Because God made us, God knows us best. God's laws reflect his wisdom and reflect his knowledge about men and women. So they're not simplistic, they're not a one size fits all.

I want to emphasise that in Islam, as repeated in the Qur'an many times, men and women are equal. They are equal spiritually, they're equal in their humanity, they have common parents in Adam and Eve, they have the same purpose in life, and they have the same potential to excel in the eyes of God. Muslims have had a completely different narrative to the narrative that has been here in Europe and in America. Fourteen centuries ago, Islam gave women the right to an education. These are things that are explicitly stated by the Prophet Muhammad: women's right to own their own property even after they marry, the right to inherit, the right to political participation. In the West these things have only been afforded to women in the last two centuries or so.

Where Islamic law treats men and women differently is where it takes into account their real differences, their biological differences, our psychological differences. I would contend with Mary Ann over her statement that our brains are the same, because I've been reading the book *The Female Brain* by Dr

Louann Brizendine, and she very clearly talks about how scientists have documented an astonishing array of structural, chemical, genetic, hormonal and functional brain differences between men and women. Dr Leonard Sax, in his book *Why Gender Matters*, describes the 1960s to the 1990s as dark ages when it comes to our understanding of gender roles, because it was politically incorrect at that time to say that boys and girls, men and women, have innate differences.

I see the roles of men and women as complementing each other. We're not in competition with each other, and I think that's where the feminist movement in this country has kind of gone astray. We have different roles, we are not interchangeable – to say we are is to demean our humanity.

LINDA WOODHEAD, Professor of Sociology of Religion and co-organiser of the Westminster Faith Debates

I can vividly remember when it was announced in November 1992 that the vote had been passed for the ordination of women within the Church of England. There was much rejoicing and high hopes. It was a very significant event, or so it seemed.

More than 20 years later, I feel rather differently. I'm not so sure it was a cause for celebration, and I don't think it has advanced the Church of England, my church, a great deal. It may even have been counterproductive for women. I say this even though I remain a feminist and am as committed to the cause of women's equality as ever.

Gender difference is a really hard issue to get a grip on. There are all sorts of ways in, and there are all sorts of slippery words like equality and difference that we've been trying to pin down. One way that you can get some purchase on the issue is to think about gender segregation in spatial terms.

Now it so happens that Britain in 2013 does not have many formally segregated spaces. There are toilets and changing rooms.

To some extent we still segregate school-age children, and some hospital wards separate men and women. But compared with even 50 years ago there are few 'men only' or 'women only' spaces left.

When I was young I attended a Catholic convent school for three years. It was an entirely female world. I loved that, and never thought of it as segregated. It felt absolutely normal and was very empowering – women could and did occupy all the positions of power, and do all the things that men could do. I think it's well known that all-girls schools have very good outcomes for girls. So why do we feel good about that but maybe not about the gentlemen's club?

Here I think you have to make a distinction between majorities and minorities. Sociologists use the term 'ascribed minorities' to refer to groups which may have a numerical dominance but are not dominant in society. Women are an ascribed minority. I think one of the criteria we employ when we make a judgement about whether it's okay to segregate by gender is whether doing so helps a minority or further hinders it. I think that's why we may feel fine about all-girls schools, possibly less about all-boys schools, and much less about all-male clubs – because men are the majority and women the (ascribed) minority.

It's good for minorities to have spaces because they shelter and protect and offer a breathing space for people on whom life may bear down rather hard. Anyone can imagine that if you're a black person in a white culture it can feel liberating to be with people of your own colour. It's often the same with cultures, age cohorts and gender. You can breathe a sigh of relief and talk about common experiences and things 'they' wouldn't naturally understand. So allowing different treatment for different groups, especially minorities, is not just about oppression and domination. It can simply be about giving space for people to play by their rules on their own terms.

Then again, not all separate spaces are necessarily good spaces. If women are being allowed separate space, is it the very back of the hall where you can't see and hear as well, is it a horrible little cut-off corner, or is it the front? Or in a home,

71

who's got the biggest office space if you've both got jobs, and who's left to use the kitchen or the shed?

So I come back to why I feel rather rueful about the ordination of women priests in the Anglican Church since 1992. In some ways I think the Catholic Church has done better by *not* allowing women and *not* allowing married men to be ordained, because however wrong this may be, in practice it means that the priesthood has become smaller and smaller, so that now it can't control everything. What's happened in the Anglican Church is the opposite. Now anyone who wants to be a serious Anglican has got to be ordained. But in being ordained they enter into male spaces and live by the logic of that space. Women clergy are less well paid and half of them aren't paid at all. So they're not on equal terms, they don't share the space fairly, and they haven't been able to change the culture. So their voice and their ability to be distinctive has been lessened compared with Catholic women, who have not been ordained and are still vocal and campaigning and doing creative and interesting things on their own terms. And that's why I feel sad about what's happened.

DISCUSSION

Culture and context

Charles Clarke I'd like to kick off by asking whether it's a problem from your point of view that there is a dislocation between the views of the public on many of these questions and the views of church or synagogue or mosque leaderships. Is it a problem that there's even within a particular faith a distinction between the views of the people of that faith and the people who are leading that faith?

Linda Woodhead I feel strongly that situation is wrong because if you have a national church like the Church of England with the privileges of establishment [being the official state church], then it should be the Church of *England*, so to be completely adrift from what most English people, including Anglicans, believe is particularly problematic.

Rod Thomas   I think that we can overstate the problem. There was a big outcry when the Church of England refused to accept that women could be made bishops last November. I totally understand that, if you construe that debate solely in terms of whether there should be women bishops or not. But I want to point out that the issue at stake was not that. It was about how much space should be allowed for the minority who disagree in order to be able to operate with a degree of freedom within the Anglican Church. So I think you will find that this disjunction between public perception and Church of England policy would disappear overnight if the Church of England actually came up with a solution as to how to do it.

Mary Ann Sieghart   I think it's a huge issue actually. I think a lot of people feel very alienated by what's gone on in the Church of England. They feel alienated by the Roman Catholic Church, and the younger they are the more alienated they feel. I don't think young people who feel passionately about discrimination are going to change their views as they get older. And I think part of the problem is that the world has changed but the word of scripture hasn't. If you take a very scriptural view of your religion then you get really stuck. And I think you should also be asking yourself, what is it in the Bible that we should be strictly adhering to? I mean, what about Leviticus? Do you believe that a disabled man shouldn't be allowed to approach the altar? Do you eat prawn cocktails and wear polycotton shirts? You're not allowed to wear two fibres together according to Leviticus … The Qur'an still gives daughters only half the inheritance of sons and says that a woman's testimony is worth only half that of a man's. It doesn't seem very equal to me.

Harvey Belovski   I agree with Mary Ann on this. First of all I don't eat prawn cocktails and I don't wear mixed fibres in my clothes. Having said that, I think the dissonance between modernity and tradition is an acute problem for all religious leaders, establishment or not. We're not tied to the word in quite the same way that perhaps Christians are because we have an oral, evolving, interpretive tradition. It has to be within certain parameters. I think we have to try to distinguish between those things which genuinely respond to gender distinctions, and those which are tinged with historic discrimination which need to be re-evaluated.

Mary Ann Sieghart   So would you be happy with a female rabbi?

Harvey Belovski   I think that, as the world is at the moment, no. The liberal Jewish world which has a completely different understanding of the binding nature of scripture and of the oral tradition understandably has gone on that route. That's part of the tension.

Fatima Barkatulla   I would like to address the examples that Mary Ann gave. There is this kind of caricaturing of the Sharia [Islamic law] and what I'd like to encourage everyone to do is to always look a little bit deeper. So yes, I will inherit half the amount that my brother will inherit from our parents, but when it comes to my wealth it's for me, me and nobody else, whereas my brother will have to provide for his mother, his sisters, any sisters that are unmarried, his own wife, his own family. There's actually a lot of wisdom behind it. A woman's testimony, that's very much depending on what case it is. There are situations when one woman's testimony weighs much more than ten men's testimonies. So we can't just pick little examples out of context.

Now your question about popular opinion. There is an element of religion that's supposed to be timeless, and I feel that's what attracts people to Islam. So we see that there are about 5,000 people coming to Islam every year in Britain and the majority of them are women. I think that's because we don't think of popular opinion as a way to shape our religion.

Complementarity

James Grimshaw   I'm from Graveney School. I've heard a lot of talk about the differences between men and women. But even if there are common differences, surely there would be some exceptions in both genders. Some men may not be good leaders, just as some women may not be good mothers, so surely the exceptions to these rules should be allowed the space to be who they are, for example the opportunity to be a leader.

Ruth Preston   I'm from King's College, London. I'm part of a church which believes in complementarity and I wholeheartedly agree with it. I think there are principles in scripture that give some men certain responsibilities. However, I really do appreciate the feelings of Mary Ann because I live in a late modern world where women are given the same opportunity as men and for me it is all about opportunities. Therefore the way I tackle gender issues in my church is to develop ways in which women can use their skills – worship, leading, preaching, teaching, seminars and so on – while still respecting complementarity. Do you think that greater work for opportunities for women in leadership would help express equality and complementarity?

Mary Ann Sieghart   I think James in the front here made a very good point. I hated dolls, I used to play football and climb trees and I was a real tomboy, and I hate the sort of lazy generalisation of 'women are like this, men are like that'. There may be on average some differences between women and men, but there is a huge overlap and there are lots of women who are more like men than some men are, and quite a few men who are more like women than some women are. The idea that I shouldn't be allowed a position of leadership in my church because of some sort of lazy manipulation of averages actually makes me very cross. Women have made very good presidents, prime ministers, CEOs, head teachers, editors. There's only one area in which they're not allowed to lead, and that's in some religions. And

I also want to talk about scripture. The culture then was very different. I don't see why two thousand years on we have still to be behaving the way they behaved then.

Rod Thomas It's just worth pointing out that much of what's written in the New Testament on men's and women's roles in the church is based on creation principles, and therefore thinking about what the creation principle was is quite important. We all know people exactly as you've described, Mary Ann. I think what it all boils down to is asking ourselves the question whether we believe in revealed religion or whether we believe in religion that we ourselves have the power to modify as time goes on. If you believe that God has revealed certain things and that is the authority that holds you within the religion, then even though you can see lots of reasons for making exceptions in particular cases, there is a generality of revealed truth that needs to be expressed in the way you organise yourselves.

Ruth asked the question about should we provide more opportunities for complementary ministry to be expressed by women and I totally agree with that. I firmly believe in extending women's ministry within our individual churches. I have two women on my team of five and I'm all in favour of that.

Lindsay Simmonds I'm from The Gender Institute, LSE. It seems to me that there's a systematic use here of the word 'roles', whereas, if you look in scripture, men and women just do things. They're not necessarily ascribed roles. I think there's a problem here with the difference between de-scription and pre-scription.

Tom Thorp I'm from the Tony Blair Faith Foundation. What about quality? I found in my own faith that a lot of the time women preachers, women priests give much better sermons and have a much better idea of theology than some men that I've heard talking. They actually do a much better job, pastoral job, as well as leading services and doing these roles which men are meant to be better at. We had that question earlier about the exceptions to the rules. When women are better at doing the job than men why should they not be allowed to take on that position?

The Golden Rule

Mary Ann Sieghart   No one has yet dealt with my question about the golden rule at the beginning. Suppose it were the other way round in the Anglican Church. Suppose I was saying, 'I couldn't have you as a bishop telling me what to do, that's disgusting. I want special arrangements because I would feel tainted if I had a bishop who was male who told me what to do.' How would you feel?

Rod Thomas   I think if it was expressed in the terms you've just expressed it in I'd feel pretty embittered, but I don't think anybody is expressing it in those terms.

Mary Ann Sieghart   Quite a lot of your allies do actually, and it's how it makes us feel.

Rod Thomas   Now wait a minute, Mary Ann. I don't think anybody is suggesting that we're 'disgusted' at this, which is the terminology you've used. We're simply talking about appropriateness of roles and the complementarity of roles.

Mary Ann Sieghart   Okay, so let's take out the disgust and just have it completely the other way round. Suppose that at the moment it's only women bishops and a few men have been allowed to be priests and people like me are saying, 'I don't think men should be allowed to be bishops simply because I don't want to have a male bishop anywhere in my diocese and it would feel wrong to me.' So, saying it in a very civilised way, how would you feel about that?

Rod Thomas   Well, I would say that wasn't a theological

argument and therefore it was irrelevant to consider it. The point
is that if I was to say I don't want a male bishop anywhere in my
diocese, the question would be why, why don't I want that? And
if the reason was because I believed that God had said that within
his church he wanted us to model particular types of behaviour
that were gender specific, then if I believed in that revelation I
would want to be faithful to it.

Is God male or female?

Patrick Morrow   I'm from the Council of Christians and Jews. I
think in this discussion we might be deluding ourselves if we don't
make some reference back to the statistics right at the beginning
from Linda, which show just how huge the majority of people is
who think that God is male. Surely the people of faith on the panel
have to have some suggestions as to how they can reform their own
traditions so that it is clear on the ground that God is not male, for
all the three faiths represented here do not believe that God is male.

Fatima Barkatullah   In Islam God is neither male nor female
and that's something very clear in the Qur'an. Nothing is like
God. We don't believe that we were created in the image of God.
We have the names and attributes of God, which are names and
attributes that God has told us about himself, and I think they
help us to relate to him. We refer to him as 'him' because that's
how he refers to himself, but that doesn't mean that God is male.

Lindsay Simmonds   I'm from The Gender Institute, LSE.
How would Rod especially feel if when he prayed the word was
'Mother' rather than 'Father', and what effect do you really think
that has on Christianity in general?

Rod Thomas   If the Bible left me free to decide those things then
I would be relaxed about it, but the Bible doesn't. Because I believe
in revealed religion, and the Bible tells me to think of God as

Father, then I don't see myself as free to think in terms of Mother.

Andrew Worthley   I'm a barrister and lecturer. To what degree does the presence of intersex [individuals who are neither straightforwardly male nor female biologically] in society problematise this very binary discussion that there has been so far?

Linda Woodhead   I think that the Christian tradition plays with gender in really interesting ways historically, and that for most of Christian history Christians, actually like Greek thought, didn't have as clear a view as we modern people do of men and women as distinct. From an Aristotelian view there is just one kind of human, the man. Men get kind of 'cooked' a bit longer in the womb and are more formed, women a bit less, but with effort women can become male. There's a lot of talk in the Christian tradition, in the early church and the medieval period, about female men of God.

Part of the point about celibacy and spiritual disciplines is that women attain equal stature with men. And actually modern Christianity has closed down a lot on the open, malleable possibility of gender roles, just as modern society did by adopting a particular medicalised understanding of 'there's a biological female and there's a biological male', as if that defines our humanity. In its fullness, the Christian tradition is much more experimental and much more interesting, and I think we lose a lot in forgetting that.

SOME MEDIA REACTION

More Muslims than Anglicans approve of the Church of England's current policies towards women, a new poll suggests ... Professor Linda Woodhead, Director of the Religion and Society Programme at Lancaster University, said that the poll results showed 'that the Churches are seriously out of step, not only with society, but with their own members.'

Ed Thornton, *Church Times*, 8 March 2013

Summary: **WHAT HAVE WE LEARNED?** by **LINDA WOODHEAD**

- One thing this debate shows is that it is impossible to disentangle the issue of how religions should treat men and women from the wider issue of just how important gender differences really are.

- On one side of this debate is Mary Ann Sieghart, who argues that there are no essential differences between men and women which would justify religions treating them differently. On the other side are Fatima Barkatullah and Rod Thomas who argue, on the basis of the Qur'an and the Bible respectively, that there are very significant differences between men and women, and that these differences ought to be respected. Harvey Belovski takes a position near to this, but is more willing to say that some religious practices may be influenced by their historical contexts, and may be discriminatory in an unhelpful way. Linda Woodhead thinks that there are differences between men and women which may justify different treatment, but that these differences are created by social and cultural inequalities rather than being essential and unchanging.

- Another thing this debate shows is that a lot depends on where you take your authority from. If you rely primarily on Qur'an and Bible, you are likely to end up with a different view from those who rely on experience, science and their own judgement. On the other hand, there are plenty of scientific writings – including a great deal of socio-biology – which insists that there are significant differences between men and women. And other scientists disagree. There are also liberal readings of Bible and Qur'an which stress gender equality, and conservative ones which stress gender difference. There is no single body of evidence or scripture that can settle the issue, and in the end one's views about gender difference seem to have as much to do with broader religious, ethical commitments and life stances as with reason and evidence.

- What the evidence does show, however, is that a majority of adults in Great Britain don't agree that religions are justified in treating men and women differently, especially when that means allowing men to be leaders but not women. Does that mean they also deny essential differences between the sexes? Possibly, although it is hard for any survey to really gauge that. We do know, however, that many of those who oppose same-sex marriage do so on the grounds that marriage should only be between a man and a woman – which implies that there is something irreducible and important about gender difference. But less than a third of the population think this – which may be quite a good measure of how many think men and women are significantly different (see Debate 5).

- So we have a situation in Britain today where religious leaders and official religious teachings treat men and women differently, but where most religious and non-religious people believe that this is wrong. As Charles Clarke says, this is a difficult position for religious leaders to maintain, and it may be one reason why traditional religions are losing support among some younger people. After all, those who think that men and women should be treated equally are just as principled in holding this view as those who think the opposite – and it is difficult to belong to a religion which contradicts one's fundamental ethical commitments, whichever side you are on.

DISCUSSION QUESTIONS

1. Mary Ann Sieghart said, '... our brains aren't different and our hearts aren't different and our souls aren't different. In every respect that pertains to religion we're exactly the same.' Is she right?

2. Lindsay Simmonds from the audience drew a distinction between described roles and prescribed roles. 'If you look in scripture men and women just do things' differently, rather than 'being' fundamentally different. Do you agree?

3. Does religious leadership need more fundamental reform than just opening the doors to women?

4. Do you think it is right to think of God as male, female, both or neither?

5. Do you think that the view you hold of God as male, female, both or

neither necessarily affects how you think about men and women and their nature and differences?

6. Fatima Barkatulla said that 'we don't think of popular opinion as a way to shape our religion.' Should religion take account of what people think (including its own followers), and does it matter if religion is out of step with the prevailing culture, especially with regard to gender?

RESOURCES

View the debates on www.faithdebates.org.uk.

Reform, whose Director Rod Thomas was one of the debate speakers, lists various resources explaining their approach to gender difference and women's ministry: http://reform.org.uk/resources/media-downloads/ src/category/god-s-way-women.

For an alternative evangelical Church of England viewpoint, Fulcrum has a searchable archive of articles: http://www.fulcrum-anglican.org.uk/ articles.cfm.

Link to the interview with Jimmy Carter about women and religion: http://swampland.time.com/2013/06/23/jimmy-carter-a-sunday-interview/.

Michael Kaufman, *The Woman in Jewish Law and Tradition* (Jason Aronson Publishers, 1993). A sensitive and comprehensive examination of the complementary roles that men and women have in private and public Jewish life.

Linda Woodhead, 'Gender differences in religious practice and significance', in James Beckford and N. J. Demerath III (eds), *The Sage Handbook of the Sociology of Religion* (Sage, 2007), pp. 550–70 (available via Google scholar). An introduction to thinking about gender and religion.

CHAPTER FOUR

What's a traditional family and do we need it?

Do we need the traditional family? Quick answer: we can't have it. It's been swept away by social and economic change. And even what we see as being a traditional model for a married couple with children is a short-lived creation of the twentieth century.
Ronald Hutton

The traditional family, where the focus is on lifelong marriage vows, a definite decision to be a couple with a future and a parental commitment to each other and to any children who may come out of that relationship, is a structure which, although having its flaws, although it's not always working, is something that we need.
Andrew Goddard

It's very clear that most people still value family life, they want to do the right thing by each other, they want to put their children first, they're looking for long-term relationships and they value commitment. But those commitments don't always take the form of what we think of as a traditional family.
Rosalind Edwards

Opening comment by **CHARLES CLARKE**

'Hard-working families' are a staple of modern political rhetoric. 'Family values' are a regular source of political appeal. Policies, for example at

Budget time, are scrutinised from the point of view of their propensity to promote marriage.

Beyond the rhetoric, social policy is beset by discussions about appropriate family relationships, for example by reference to the number of bedrooms a family needs to receive welfare payments, or which family relationships should entitle an individual to join their immigrant relative in this country.

Article 8 of the European Convention of Human Rights gives a 'Right to respect for private and family life', which is constantly the subject of important battles of interpretation.

This debate sought to illuminate what is meant by 'family' in this range of different but important contexts which have changed greatly over time.

At the core of the idea of family is the group of people who bring up a child and give her/him a social context and support. The parents will usually be the most important, though this is significantly qualified by the circumstances in which, for whatever reason, one or both of the parents is absent or incapable of support. For the child, some source of unqualified support or love is an essential rock for their development.

And then a range of others have great significance, siblings, grandparents, 'nannies', aunts and uncles, 'godmothers' and 'godfathers', other significant adults will all be important, in different ways and at different times. A child's own friends and peer group are also extremely influential.

The idea of the 'traditional family' tends to give much greater, sometimes even unique, significance to the family relationships of biological mother and father and often to give almost no value to the importance of other relationships.

This is difficult to sustain when the pattern of modern life has changed so that this biological relationship is an increasingly small proportion of modern families. The rate of change is dramatic, as the opening statistical presentation shows beyond question. Divorce, social mobility, economic change and longevity have changed the pattern of modern families.

The challenge for policy-makers is to find answers which strengthen and uphold the enduring importance of family relationships, particularly for children, while reflecting the true make-up of modern families.

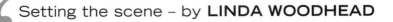

Setting the scene – by **LINDA WOODHEAD**

The family has been changing fast. As Figure 1 shows, there has been a big drop in the number of married women – from 74% in the 1970s to 47% in 2011. In part this is because of divorce, but also because more women are choosing not to marry. Some remain single and, as Figure 1 shows, others cohabit rather than marry. This makes a difference to the unit within which children are born and raised. The ONS survey on lone parents (2011) shows that the number of lone-parent families has more than tripled from 8% in 1971 to 26% in 2011.

ONS 2011 General Lifestyle survey

● **Number of women aged 18 to 49 who were married has fallen from 74% in 1979 to 47% in 2011**

● **Number of women who are single (never married) has risen from 18% in 1979 to 43% in 2011**

● **Number of women 18–49 cohabitating has tripled, from 11% in 1979 to 34% in 2011.**

Figure 1: The changing 'family'.

So if we think of a traditional family as 'married with children', how many such families are there in Britain today? Figure 2 gives the figures from the latest census for England and Wales, carried out in 2011. It shows that under half of households now contain a married couple, and that around a quarter of the population live in a traditional family (8% with one child, 18% with two).

A smaller proportion of people live in traditional families today than in the past – we know that in 1961 about 38% of people lived in a traditional family, and that within living memory it was much more of a norm to be raised in such a setting. There was also much more shame attached to any deviation from that norm – to being a single parent, an 'illegitimate' child and so on.

2011 Census, England and Wales

44.3% of the population lives in married couple households, of which

10.4% are married persons with no children

8.2% are married persons with 1 dependent child

17.9% are married persons with 2 or more dependent children

7.9% are married persons with non-dependent children

Figure 2

Given that a minority of people now live in, or even have a direct experience of, a traditional family, have our attitudes towards it changed? And what do we think constitutes a 'family' these days? In our YouGov survey we gave people a list of options of what might constitute a family.

Not surprisingly, nearly everyone agrees that a married couple with children is a family. More surprising is the way in which there is still widespread agreement that it's biological/ genetic bonds and kinship which constitute a family unit. We asked about relationships which have more to do with emotional ties than biological ones. Figure 3 shows that fewer people regard these as proper families, but that significant numbers do.

What's a family?

A married couple with children – all agree

An unmarried couple with children 89%

A lone parent with at least one child 87%

A married couple without children 72%

Siblings who live together 71%

A same-sex couple in a civil partnership with children 70%

An unmarried couple without children 52%

A same-sex couple in a civil partnership 47%

Any two or more people who care for each other 39%

Figure 3: YouGov for Westminster Faith Debates 2013

Most people these days think it's perfectly acceptable *not* to start a biological family of one's own. When we asked whether more women never having children is good or bad, 72% say good or 'neither good nor bad'. But most people still think children need families, preferably with a father and a mother – though the European Values Survey, which has been asking a question about this since the 1980s, finds that attitudes have been changing, with fewer people now thinking that a child needs a father and a mother to grow up happily. When we asked whether more single women having children without a male partner is good or bad, 30% say neither, and 58% say bad. When asked whether more gay and lesbian couples raising children is good or bad, 24% say good, 31% bad and 39% neither.

You might think religious people would be more conservative. Our survey finds they're not. For example, 46% of Catholics, 51% of Baptists, and 48% of Jewish people consider a same-sex couple in a civil partnership without children to be a family, compared with 47% of the general population.

If we think in terms of a spectrum of views about what constitutes a family, with the view that biological bonds make a family at one end (the biological view), and the view that bonds of care and affection make a family at the other (the affective view), what sort of characteristics predict whether a person takes the first view?

The two most important factors which predict whether you think a family is biological are: (a) voting Conservative, and (b) being male. The next most important are (c) being in the minority of religious believers who take their main authority from God or scripture and religious teachings (Baptists and Muslims score highest on this), and (d) being over 65.

The increasing use of assisted reproductive technologies such as sperm and egg donation are complicating the whole picture further. In some cases new reproductive options make it harder to say who counts as a 'real' parent, and the issue about the relative importance of affective and biological bonds becomes more pressing.

It's also interesting to reflect that the churches, which tend today to exalt the biological family, also have a tradition of taking the affective or spiritual family more seriously. Jesus asked the question 'Who is my mother and who are my brothers?' and gave the controversial answer, 'Whoever does the will of my Father in heaven is my brother and sister and mother' (Matthew 12.48, 50). This helped inspire traditions of celibacy and monasticism in some churches. The human family was exchanged for a spiritual family – God is the ultimate 'Father', but 'Pope' and 'Abbot' also mean 'father'. Christians sometimes call one another 'brothers' and 'sisters', and the church becomes 'the Christian family'. There are parallels in some, but not all, religions, which, as this debate will show, take different attitudes towards the importance of the biological family.

THE DEBATE

RONALD HUTTON, Professor of History at Bristol University[1]

Do we need the traditional family? Quick answer: we can't have it. It's been swept away by social and economic change. And even what we see as being a traditional model for a married couple with children is a short-lived creation of the twentieth century.

Before the twentieth century, being a married couple with children meant a totally different set of things. Until the nineteenth century, by the time most children reached the age of 12 they'd lost at least one parent. In other words, most people were products of broken homes, but broken by death rather than by desertion or divorce. Practically everybody had to work across most of society and most children left home to do so (for ever) at

[1] Professor Ronald Hutton has published extensively on the history of Paganism and on the British Isles in the sixteenth and seventeenth centuries. His recent books include *A Brief History of Britain, 1485–1660* (Robinson, 2011) and *Blood and Mistletoe: The history of the Druids in Britain* (Yale University Press, reprint 2011).

the age of 12 or 13. When you put together back-breaking daily labour, hypothermia for much of the year, chronic malnutrition and low-level illness, you have low libidos in most people. Puberty doesn't happen for most of the population until the age of 17 or 18. You're not going to get gymslip mums because they can't become mums. And people live in small communities where the choice of marital or sexual partners is very limited indeed.

Now jump to the present. You have a situation in which for the first time in history across the western world people are expected to make partnerships and if possible keep them for decades and decades instead of a few years of expected life. They're expected to keep their children at home and look after them and discipline them until they're 16 or 17, and they're expected to have a common social life which on the whole women and men didn't have until the nineteenth and twentieth centuries. And they're expected both to work. The pressures are enormous and unprecedented, so no wonder the family is falling to bits or under pressure at present, and forming new patterns and alliances to cope.

So how does traditional religion relate to this? In Europe, traditional over the long span means two different types of religion, Paganism and Christianity. And they're very different. Ancient Paganism regarded marriage as a civil contract, which could be liquidated or broken if one party really desired to get out of it. Sex was regarded as something to be enjoyed to the full providing there was a certain amount of caution and restraint about it. Providing that you were the active partner, you were enjoying it and you were showing due moderation in the number of partners you chose, that was it.

Christianity was very different. Christianity ambiguously prized both celibacy and marriage. As the years went on, Catholicism tended to regard celibacy as an ideal state, and Protestantism marriage as an ideal state, but what they had in common was a quite unprecedented hostility to sex outside marriage of any kind, and over the years increasingly towards gay, lesbian or bisexual unions. This was not the case in the ancient world.

89

Christian morality has today become a lot harder to make fit with society than before. If you're marrying somebody for life and it means decades, it's a whole different deal. And likewise you have the abilities that people have to meet new partners of all different types, and sex drives out of all proportion to those people had before the twentieth century. On the other hand, the fact that Christian morality is a lot harder to fit the reality now may make it all the more admirable and strenuous and praiseworthy as an ideal to which certain people would wish to live up and perhaps, should they wish, hold up to others as an ideal. But others might say that the older, more secular, more pragmatic, more practical, ancient and Pagan way of looking at sex and marriage might be a handy and more flexible model to which to return if we're going to bother with faith at all.

POLLY TOYNBEE, Columnist for the *Guardian* newspaper[2]

The YouGov survey discussed by Linda shows how tolerant people have become, how very flexible in their attitudes to what is a family. Nevertheless, plenty of other polls show us that the romantic idea remains pretty strongly embedded in most people. Your ideal is that you will meet your perfect partner, that you will get married, stay together for life, have children, that you will love your partner forever and your partner will love you forever and your children will miraculously love you forever too. That remains the ideal. It's a very good one, a very good way of bringing up children. We know from all sorts of social research that very happy families are very good for children.

But the trouble is that life, as people well know and

[2] Polly Toynbee is a columnist for the *Guardian* newspaper. In the 1990s she was the BBC's Social Affairs editor. She is a former President of the British Humanist Association. Her books include *Hard Work: Life in low-pay Britain* (Bloomsbury, 2003) and *Dogma and Disarray – Cameron at Half-Time* (Granta, 2012, co-authored with David Walker).

understand, is very difficult and complicated and human beings are difficult and it doesn't often work out that way. These days people are freer to make choices. They regret it when a marriage breaks up but they recognise that it wasn't necessarily better to lock people up together. So we don't necessarily live in conventional families any more. A quarter of children grow up in single-parent families for all sorts of different and complicated reasons.

Nevertheless there remains a strong political pull on the right to blame single parents. You hear Iain Duncan Smith saying over and over again that marriage is the answer, people wouldn't be poor if they were married, which is partly true because we still have a society where the economy makes it very difficult for women to bring up children on their own. So the state is involved in this whether it has a moral view or not.

There are all kinds of reasons why marriages break up. Very often women are quite right to walk away and take their children from marriages where men maybe use drugs, drink and gamble, or abuse, or may just be very bad fathers. A father isn't always a good thing, and not all mothers are good either. I think there is a great deal of danger in that this government has decided that benefits are going to be paid to fathers. If it's a bad father who doesn't hand the money over, lots of mothers will be forced to leave and take their children with them because otherwise they can't support the family. All of the research shows it's much better to give the money to the mother if you want to get it spent on the children in the right kind of way.

I think there are limits to the state's influence. The idea of a marriage bonus in the tax system is ludicrous – the idea that a hundred or even a couple of a hundred pounds a year is going to make people get married or stay married when we know that they get divorced at phenomenal cost to themselves. But I think there are things the state can do to support marriage. It used to be that only the rich could afford to get divorced. Now it tends to be people with least money where the financial pressure simply breaks people apart. When new and bigger cuts come in, that is going to split families apart in a really big way, taking hundreds and thousands of people out of their communities to places far away where they have no ties whatever.

Good secure housing keeps families together. The state can help with paying for Relate and mediation services if things are going wrong. It can provide affordable childcare – virtually all families now need at least an income and a half to have a reasonable standard of living, and childcare's part of that. Good pay and a living wage would give fathers more time to have time with their families, and make life easier for mothers too.

I think every politician praises the family but the important question in the end is to be realistic about what the state can and can't do to support families. It can't change social and moral attitudes and values. But the state can do the best it can to support families wherever they are and whatever shape they are.

ANDREW GODDARD, Associate Director of the Kirby Laing Institute for Christian Ethics[3]

We've seen the statistics. Let me add another. There's been a massive rise in births outside marriage. Between 1600 and the 1960s that fluctuated between about 1% and 9% of live births. It's now at 47% of live births. In the last 30 or 40 years, that's a major change.

To put my cards on the table, my understanding of traditional family is similar to some of what came out I think in the YouGov survey. It's a network of both voluntary and involuntary relationships based on birth and based on marriage. That might be a narrow network sort of nuclear family or it might be a wider network, the extended family. And it's a network where children

[3] Dr Andrew Goddard lectures on Christian ethics. At the Kirby Laing Institute for Christian Ethics he focuses on marriage and sexual ethics. He serves on the leadership team of Fulcrum, a network of Anglican evangelicals, and is an honorary canon of Winchester Cathedral.

are brought up by their biological parents who've decided to commit themselves to each other in lifelong exclusive marriage as the relational base and the context for having and raising children.

Let me explain why Christians have been supportive of the traditional family, why they see it as good for those involved, particularly for children, but also good for wider society. You might expect from the Christian scriptures there to be more questioning of family. The pictures of family life in the Bible are brutally honest, right from the beginning in the creation stories at the beginning of Genesis. As Linda said, Jesus even talks about hating father and mother in order to follow him. And so that's a warning about how family can become an idol, a false god, an ultimate value when it shouldn't be ultimate.

So why have Christians seen the traditional family pattern as the norm or the gold standard of family? Firstly, family language is used in relation to God. Jesus taught his disciples to pray 'Our Father'. Isaiah compares God to a nursing mother or a comforting mother. Both Jewish and Christian teaching sees the relationship between man and woman in marriage as in some sense reflecting God's relationship with us. Secondly, it's because of an understanding about how humans flourish: we are made by God to be social creatures in an ordered creation and we flourish best in respecting that order.

So the question becomes, 'What patterns of parenting and pair-bonding best reflect the character of God as these traditions believe in him?'

And I think traditional families point to certain constraints, certain givens. We are embedded in some involuntary relationships, most basically we don't choose our own parents. But it's also rooted in making decisions to commit to other people. The family is the most formative structure in learning to be social beings. The traditional family in theory and often in practice provides a structure which stresses the importance of continuity, commitment, security, stability, love and sacrifice for the good of others.

Thirdly, there's also a fundamental concern for the weak and the vulnerable. What structures offer the best environment for the weakest? And I think there's much evidence that the traditional family works best. For example, by the age of 15, 45% of children today do not live with both their birth parents. Where parents are still together when the child is 15, 97% of those parents are married. So I think we need to look at the evidence about what is good and best for children.

All these reasons point back to the fundamental point which is an understanding of promising and embodying committed, self-giving love for others. I believe the traditional family, with a focus on lifelong marriage vows and a parental commitment to each other and to any children who may come out of that relationship, is a structure which, although having its flaws, although it's not always working, is something that we still need.

ROSALIND EDWARDS, Professor of Sociology at the University of Southampton[4]

When we think of a traditional family we've not only got an image of the husband and the wife living together with their biological children, we've also got an image of the husband being the breadwinner and the wife being the homemaker. This image evokes stability and continuity; comfort and being together; togetherness, obligations, reciprocity; somebody always being there for you, and so on. But it's quite a narrow view of family, and it's become clear from the figures which Linda presented that this is not actually the family that many of us live with any more.

We've not only got declining marriage rates, people who get married are older than previously. There's the rise in the

[4] Professor Rosalind Edwards has researched and published widely on family life and policies. She is an elected member of the Academy of Social Sciences and sits on the Methods and Infrastructure Committee of the Economic and Social Research Council.

proportion of children born outside marriage, and the proportion of lone mothers growing steadily. Stepfamilies are common.

Some people would argue that this is very good, they see the demise of the traditional family as an escape from oppressive relationships or unequal relationships, and think that we can replace that with purer, more democratic relationships.

Others view these changes as much darker. They see people becoming more individualistic and pursuing their own selfish ends, leaving a trail of broken relationships, damaged children and a broken society.

My view is that that debate about whether changes in the family are good or bad is confused. It assumes that change in the *form* of the family is the same as change in the *substance* of people's lives. Instead, my own and other people's research reveals a more complex picture not only of continuity as well as change, but of change *as* continuity.

It's very clear that most people still value family life. They want to do the right thing by each other, they want to put their children first, they're looking for long-term relationships and they value commitment. But those commitments don't always take the form of what we think of as a traditional family. That focus on commitment and on doing the right thing, I think you could call that the wine of old family content in the bottles of new family forms.

Also, because society's changing, for families to stay the same in terms of their content they have to change. Marriage is still the most common family form but its meaning has changed. It's become unhooked from sex and from child-bearing and child-rearing. It's no longer the only respectable way to create a family, but it still remains a prevalent aim. People are doing things in a different order. They cohabit, they have children (which is why you get so many children born outside of marriage), then they save up enough money and have a big white wedding.

What people always ask is, 'Don't children do better when they're brought up in the traditional family form?' Research does often purport to show that children are better behaved and achieve more if their parents are married. I'm sorry to use jargon, but as a sociologist you have to think about what we call 'selection effects'. Today we think that the rates of teenage parenthood are high and that's often put forward as a symbol of broken Britain. But actually half a century ago teenage parents were much more common than they are today, and not seen as a problem. It's pre- and post-pregnancy disadvantage that causes poor outcomes for mother and child, not the age of becoming a mother.

To sum up, family forms continually change but much of what people want from family remains the same. Meaning continues on in ways that are very akin to those we associate with traditional family. What is new is that we have new traditions, new forms, evolving to express older values in a context in which family life changes as society changes around us.

DISCUSSION

Marriage, money and the state

Charles Clarke There seems to be a general view that the traditional family is a worthwhile ambition, as it were, but also that it is increasingly uncommon in the society that we have. So, should we as a society be trying to increase the number of people in traditional family forms, should we not be bothered about it, should we be looking at what Ros calls the wine inside the bottle rather than the form of it? And should the state take action?

Rosalind Edwards What the state should be doing is supporting people to live their lives as best they can in families, rather than trying to promote a particular family form. But the way that the state tends to do that is with an economic rationality.

Andrew Goddard I'm cautious about the state taking charge of this. I think we need to have the sort of discussion that we're having here today as a society – about how to encourage and structure commitment to one another. I think the state can look at the effect its policies have on families in terms of generating instability. Poverty is clearly one of the major challenges to maintaining family of whatever kind. I think we are odd among developed countries in having little recognition of marriage in the tax system, though I think it's right to say an extra hundred pounds isn't going to tip people.

Polly Toynbee That's an important point you raise. When there's very little money to dispose in any way, are you actually saying you think that we should have a recognition of marriage in the tax system and put money there because you think it would make a difference? If you were the Chancellor, is that where you would put that extra bit of money, or would you say the fundamental duty of the state is to protect vulnerable children wherever they are, as best we can, and in the process of course we hope to make family life easier for everybody wherever they are and easier for people to live happy family lives?

Ronald Hutton Like most parts of this debate, it's quite new to think that the state can solve many problems. What we don't want is what happened around 1980 when top politicians articulated a history of the family that was completely wrong and totally bogus, saying that the family was decomposing because of the welfare state, because traditionally parents provided for their own parents in old age, disciplined their children etc. etc.

Rosalind Edwards I think if Government made money available to cohabiting couples to have the big white wedding they might get more conversions of cohabiting couples into married couples because research with cohabiting couples does show that's what happens, they're waiting to make the big public statement, it's not a big religious statement, but it's a big celebration.

Polly Toynbee   I love the idea of the Iain Duncan Smith mass wedding!

Charles Clarke   They've already done that in North Korea haven't they?

Linda Woodhead   You're all being awfully positive about the traditional family. Don't forget that families are where the most awful things happen: spousal murder, domestic abuse and sexual abuse of children. And if we narrow everything down to say that the family is the only proper place for children to be raised, we may trap them in a setting which can be very dangerous.

Polly Toynbee   Well, I'm not sure the things that you're ascribing are necessarily to do with whether it's a traditional family or not. It's what happens in 'the household'.

Charles Clarke   The conversation's focused almost entirely on the position of children, and of course from the state's point of view the welfare of children is the core driving argument in this. But there's also the question about the importance of the family more widely. Linda's figures right at the beginning covered not only biological families but also a whole series of other relationships. The question of whether we should be trying to support such wider forms of bonding I thought was interesting.

Polly Toynbee   I thought you [referring to points made by Linda Woodhead and Andrew Goddard] said something really important and rarely said because it's a dangerous thing to say, that the family may not be the be all and end all, it's in danger of becoming an idol in itself. You often hear people very self-righteously justifying selfishness – 'I'm doing it for my family, whatever I do, how I'm getting the money, I'm not paying my taxes and whatever, I'm doing it for my family.' You can put up a fortress round the family as a way of not thinking about what's for the good of the wider society.

Peter Stevenson I operate as a pastor down at the Elephant and Castle, which gives me the joy of an international congregation. From an African perspective there are aunties and there are papas and there are brothers, and I haven't a clue whether they're related to each other but we are in a sense a family. But one thing that does bring them all together, and that we haven't spoken about, is the way story brings all of these things together as family. If we share the story with each other then we're part of each other. And the word that I haven't heard anybody express yet is respect. I wonder, is there a breakdown of respect which is breaking down other things?

Elizabeth Oldfield I direct the think tank Theos. I was fascinated to hear Andrew and Polly really expressing quite a similar sentiment about, not the traditional family in a very precisely delineated way, but a couple committed in a long-term way to bringing up a family, as being a really good thing, and perhaps the best thing that we should be seeking for. But I wonder if one of the reasons why that surprised me is that we've lost the moral language on this subject in society simply because that's such a difficult thing for so many people to achieve, and that people for whom that hasn't been possible can't help but feel imperfect or judged even by beginning to use this language. I think it's important that we do talk about the good, that we do talk about the best, but how do we do it in a way that includes people rather than excludes them?

Polly Toynbee I think you're absolutely right and that is a great dilemma. Whatever it is, we all have the fairy tale that we're born and brought up with, the idea of the romance that lasts for ever. It's not necessarily about whether you're married with a certificate; it's about finding 'the one' and being happy together with 'the one' for ever. It runs so strongly through all of our culture, it's so deeply ingrained in us from a very young age, that inevitably when it doesn't work out that way for huge numbers of reasons because life is difficult, people are difficult, we're all difficult, we're all hard to live with, we're all awful a lot of the time, it does feel like a falling away from the perfect.

I do think we all are born with ideals of all different kinds. We think society should be fairer than it is, we think we should be better than we are, we should be more moral if you like because I think that is imprinted on us. I think it's what makes us social animals. But it means that we are always living with the guilt of falling away from what we know we should be and should do and that's part of the human condition. But I agree that as a society it's really important that we don't judge people according to the kinds of families that they end up living in and bringing their children up in.

Andrew Goddard   I would agree with that. As I've mentioned, Bible stories about families are quite clear about how brutal they can be and we need to be honest about the lived reality. I think we need to ask what are the structures that give social support to the best type of flourishing for people.

There's apparently a Professor Scott Stanley in Denver who has got a large sample of over a thousand cohabiting unmarried couples aged 18–35 and is looking at what are the best predictors of the stability of that relationship. And it's not necessarily having had a baby or just moving in together that has been the signal of the stability, it's actually doing something that is a conscious decision to fix a life together, so buying a house, or even just getting a pet. Obviously a baby may just arrive without being planned and you might just move in together without having a conscious decision that this is a commitment that is really long term, perhaps even lifelong. And so there is some research being done as to what are the things within non-marital relationships that are pointers to them having the sense of stability and continuity maybe more akin to what has traditionally been associated with marriage and sometimes it turns up things that maybe we don't necessarily expect.

Ronald Hutton   I want to look at respect and romance, that wonderful partnership that lies at the basis of so much of this.

We may be in a difficult position at present because of social change, and we're also in a rather tough position because we're a species that unlike most animals doesn't have seasonal mating. We can mate all the time and we are neither a species that tends naturally to make long, unbreakable unions nor are we a species that is naturally more promiscuous; we produce both patterns and that's why ever since records began the ideal of falling in love and staying in love until death do part is the human ideal, it's what we'd like to do if we are interested in romance and do want to make partnerships. But the framework you place around this need can be very different and there are basically three that have existed through time.

The first is for individuals to make a relationship work emotionally and practically, maybe with the help of friends or relations. Number two is that it's a civil contract with the state or the city or the province, and individuals owe something back to the wider community for making a relationship official and getting privileges in return. And number three is that it's a contract with a deity on certain lines that the divine has prescribed, and if you break those then you may bring about the end of the world rather faster, and you're almost certainly going to have a rather dicey fate in the afterlife if you get an afterlife. And our problem now is those three languages are hopelessly intermingled, they're not being separated out. We're doing our very best to make them co-exist on this panel now to an almost dismaying extent. But I think it helps if you're conscious of how different they really are.

SOME MEDIA REACTION

Most people in the UK think of the family as primarily a biological unit, according to research carried out for the Westminster Faith Debates.

The War Cry, 13 April 2013

Religious people take as broad a view of what constitutes a 'family' as the general population does, new research suggests. But only 21 per cent of those surveyed believe that churches are welcoming to gays, lesbians and bisexuals.

Church Times, 12 April 2013

Summary: WHAT HAVE WE LEARNED? by LINDA WOODHEAD

- We often feel that social institutions like the family are timeless, but Ronald Hutton, a historian, reminds us how much it has changed over time. What we think of today as a 'traditional family' – in which wife and husband are married to one another for a lifetime and financially support their biological children in a clean, hygienic household until the children are in their late teens or even older – is in fact something unique to the affluent, relatively disease-free, late modern societies in which we are privileged to live.

- Hutton also reminds us that, historically, we have been influenced by three very different models of marriage. The first, associated with Paganism and perhaps undergoing a revival today, views marriage as a bond freely made between two individuals. The second sees marriage – and family – as something in which the state and society have an interest, and which may be supported with financial benefits like tax breaks. The third, associated with Christianity, sees marriage and family as a God-given state, whose breakdown constitutes a grave sin.

- All three models influence us today, even though they are, strictly speaking, incompatible. We can see each one at play in this debate. Of our speakers, Andrew Goddard comes closest to defending the Christian view, though he does not speak in traditional Christian terms of marriage as indissoluble nor of the breakdown of marriage and family as sin. Polly Toynbee is most reliant on the second, state-related, view of the family. And Ros Edwards is very much aware of the personal dimensions of marriage and family, as well as the state's role.

- The problem with the Christian model, says Hutton, is that it has become so difficult to uphold today, given better health, more libido, longer lives, and more social contact. No wonder only a minority of people now experience a traditional family; it's much harder to sustain than ever before. But it still constitutes an ideal which should inspire us, say Goddard and some of the audience. We can still keep the ideal of love, care and long-term commitment, says Edwards, but we must recognise that these can be lived out in very different family structures – for example, lone-parent households and extended families. But let's not forget the role of the state in all this, says Toynbee, because it's very hard to sustain the loving commitment that a marriage needs, and the stability that children need, if you are in poverty, trapped in poor housing, or unable to access childcare.

● Finally, the discussion also suggests two further areas of debate about the family. First, the issue of whether biological or emotional/spiritual bonds are what really make a family. And second, how important the family is in relation to other institutions and forms of association – is the family our primary context of belonging, to which our ultimate loyalty is owed? Or are friends, associations, the workplace and wider society equally influential in our lives and equally worthy of our time, attention and care? It's important to set the family in wider context, and think about what role it plays in our overall vision of a good society.

DISCUSSION QUESTIONS

1. Is the 'traditional family' the ideal one for raising children, or can other kinds of family be equally good?
2. Do religious teachings about lifelong marriage still have something to offer today, given all the changes in society and human life?
3. Are Polly Toynbee and Andrew Goddard right to suggest that the family can become a kind of idol, given an ultimate value, and used as a justification for selfishness and failing to do what is best for wider society?
4. Should government provide incentives to get married and stay married, and would they do any good?
5. Do you think the family is primarily bound by biological ties, or ties of care, feeling and commitment?
6. What, if anything, is bad about the 'traditional family'?

RESOURCES

View the debate at www.faithdebates.org.uk.

www.FamilyFacts.org is an American resource on religion and the family.

Family Lives is a secular UK charity which believes in families as the foundation of society, and offers resources and non-judgemental support.

The Couple Connection is a 'do-it-yourself' relationship support service with reviews of relevant research, run by the OnePlusOne agency: www. http://thecoupleconnection.net.

The Marriage Foundation (www.marriagefoundation.org.uk) undertakes research on marriage and family breakdown in society and seeks to enable people to develop the skills to form stronger relationships.

Peter Brown, *The Body and Society* (2nd edn, Columbia University Press, 2008) is a famous survey of Pagan and Christian attitudes to sex, marriage and the family in ancient and medieval times.

Jane Ribbens McCarthy and Rosalind Edwards, *Key Concepts in Family Studies* (Sage, 2011) explains ideas, issues and the latest knowledge about families.

John Tosh, *Why History Matters* (Palgrave Macmillan, 2008, pp. 78–98) has a very good concise summary of the modern history of the British family and why it differs from popular beliefs about it.

Merry Wiesner-Hanks, *Christianity and Sexuality in the Early Modern World* (2nd edn, Routledge, 2010) offers an excellent overview of Christian attitudes to sex and marriage since ancient times.

CHAPTER FIVE
Do Christians really oppose same-sex marriage?

I shall be supporting it in the House of Lords ... I don't think this is a question about what the Catholic Church could or could not do. This is a question of what the state should and should not do.
Lord Deben (John Selwyn Gummer)

The church needs to re-evaluate the more profound question about how it includes gay people and then it will be able to sort out its position over gay marriage.
Steve Chalke

I don't think being a faithful Catholic means completely accepting and not questioning whether there's not a richer understanding of same-sex sacramental marriage that could be affirmed within faith communities.
Tina Beattie

To admit gay marriage in the Church would be to undo Christian doctrine.
John Milbank

Opening comment by **CHARLES CLARKE**

Homosexuality was first decriminalised in the United States in 1962, in the state of Illinois. California followed in 1976. Only in 2003 was it decriminalised in all US states. In the UK similar legislation was passed in England and Wales in 1967, Scotland in 1980, and

Northern Ireland in 1982, and in 2000 extended to all over 16.

The process has been long and contested and change has been justified in different ways. Some make the liberal case that society should 'tolerate' and respect behaviour otherwise seen as 'abnormal'; others argue that homosexuality is just as 'normal' as heterosexuality and should be treated accordingly.

These discussions quickly turn into wider debates, for example about how homosexuality should be taught in schools, whether gay people can work in the military, and whether gay couples can adopt children. These have all been significant political debates in which the state of public opinion has played an important role.

'Gay marriage' has become the most recent of this set of battlegrounds. In many ways it is the most conclusive, as the idea of 'marriage' confers social status and public respect, and has significance for property rights and rights in relation to children. 'Civil partnerships', established in 2004, were really designed to regularise gay relationships without according them the status of 'marriage'.

Across the world 'gay marriage' has become the badge of the 'modern' politician. This is particularly important for 'modern' Conservatives who want to signal their commitment to modern social values and discard backward-looking attitudes. That is why David Cameron has committed himself to this reform against the strong feelings of the church leaderships and many in his party. He argues that his approach will strengthen the institution of marriage which itself is a central component of a strong society.

The poll results published in this debate revealed this fundamental political truth, as 52% supported gay marriage, including narrow majorities among those who identify with the Church of England and the Catholic Church.

The arguments of the opponents, whatever their other merits or demerits as demonstrated in this debate, are not in my expectation strong enough to overturn the widespread popular approval of the idea that gay marriage should be established as an important element of our national life. The story is of a lengthy and contested process of change in the status of gay relationships, but always moving in the same direction – a change in popular attitudes, generation by generation, which has been decisive.

Setting the scene – by **LINDA WOODHEAD**

This topic is different from others in this series of debates because we're focusing on a single faith tradition, Christianity. The issue of whether same-sex marriage should be allowed is currently being debated in Parliament, and church leaders have been vocal in opposing the bill which would allow it.

But whatever their leaders say, do Christians in this country really oppose same-sex marriage? Our YouGov survey gives a clear answer: on the whole they do not. There is some variation by denomination, with Baptists and Methodists being most opposed, but Anglicans and Catholics are in favour by a small margin. If we look at religious people as a whole – all those who say they belong to a religion – opinion is evenly split among those who express a view (Figure 1). People who say they have no religion are most strongly in favour.

Should same-sex couples be allowed to get married?							
	All	No religion	Anglican	RC	Presbyterian	Methodist	Baptist	Religion TOTAL
Should	52	69	44	44	49	32	40	43
Should not	34	20	43	41	44	45	50	43
Don't know	14	11	14	15	7	23	11	14

Figure 1: YouGov for Westminster Faith Debates 2013.

Looking more broadly at the spread of all religions, Figure 2 shows that Muslims are the most opposed of all, indeed Muslims and Baptists have quite a lot in common in their attitudes to sexual morality.

All these figures are for religious adherents, that is, people who say they are 'Anglican', 'Baptist' etc. Our survey also allows us to compare these results with the responses of people who currently participate in a religious group like a church. There is

Should same-sex couples be allowed to get married?					
	All	Jewish	Hindu	Muslim	Sikh	Religion TOTAL
Should	52	52	55	29	35	43
Should not	34	38	26	59	35	43
Don't know	14	10	19	12	30	14

Figure 2: YouGov for Westminster Faith Debates 2013.

a difference, but not a very large one. Churchgoing Christians are, on the whole, slightly less likely to think that same-sex people should be allowed to get married (Figure 3).

Should same-sex couples be allowed to get married? (Churchgoers)				
	Roman Catholic	Anglican	Church of Scotland	Methodist/ Baptist	Pentecostal
Should	42	40	54	31	29
Should not	48	47	37	52	65
Don't know	10	14	9	17	6

Figure 3: YouGov for Westminster Faith Debates 2013.

Our survey also asked Christians about the reasons for their opinions on same-sex marriage, and gave them a long list of choices. Two answers jumped out as most popular on either side of the debate. A majority of those who think same-sex marriage is right give as their reason that 'People should be treated equally whatever their sexual orientation' (77%), and a majority of those who think it is wrong appeal to the fact that 'Marriage should be between a man and a woman' (79%).

From this we can conclude that people's attitudes to same-sex marriage are closely related to their views about the difference between men and women. For those who think that the sexes are equal or similar in the things that really matter, extending marriage to include unions between two people of the same sex does not seem problematic. But for those who think there are deeply significant differences between men and women, such a change undermines the very essence of marriage.

THE DEBATE

JOHN GUMMER, Lord Deben, Member of the House of Lords[1]

In a secular society, if two people of the same sex want to say that their relationship is permanent in the same sense that marriage is permanent, then I think they should be allowed to do so by the state. I don't find that difficult and I think we have to do that to make up for a very long period during which gay people were treated in a way for which we should be ashamed.

So I welcome the decision of the House of Commons to support this change and I shall be supporting it in the House of Lords.

I believe there is a clear distinction between what I as a Catholic see as marriage and what the state sees as marriage. I think it's a mistake for the church to try to pretend otherwise or for the state to pretend otherwise. One of the problems is that we have tried that fudge for too long, which is what happens when the clergyman is seen both as the registrar of the state and as the performer of the religious rite of marriage.

In the church the sacrament of marriage is something which

[1] Before joining the House of Lords John Gummer was an MP and a minister in the governments of Margaret Thatcher and John Major. He converted from Anglicanism to Roman Catholicism over the issue of authority and the power of the Church of England to act unilaterally on matters such as the ordination of women.

is reserved for one man and one woman, and that I perfectly accept. But we're not talking about sacramental marriage, we're talking about state marriage. I don't think this is a question about what the Catholic Church could or could not do. This is a question of what the state should and should not do. And it's because we have confused these two things that makes it very difficult to have a proper conversation about the issue.

So I am not making any comment whatsoever about the teaching of the Catholic Church. I am a convert so I've chosen to accept that doctrine. But what I'm saying here is that as a politician, as somebody who is responsible for the law, I have to take the view that this is not an area where the law should be enforcing rules and regulations which are perfectly proper for the church to teach but not proper for the state.

The trouble for the Church of England is it was created in order to present the morality of the state as if it were the morality of the church. Let's be clear about it. The Church of England is a political creation and the problem today for the Church of England is that it perfectly properly resents the concept that it is a political creation, but the difficulty for the Archbishop of Canterbury is by what other authority does it speak?

This is why I was a convert, because at least the Catholic Church speaks with the authority of Christ. That's what its claim is. Whereas, the Church of England speaks with an authority which derives ultimately from a political deal in order to ensure that the king could marry a divorcee, that's the history.

This is the first time in which we really are trying to have a proper conversation about the issue of same-sex marriage. Even the idea of the civil partnership was one which the Government mishandled, because it told one side that it was marriage and the other side that it wasn't marriage. Indeed I refused to vote for it, not because I was against it but because I am against fraud and that was a fraudulent presentation. And I do think that at least we now have an absolutely straight question: 'Do you accept that, given the nature of marriage in our secular society, irrespective of what marriage is for a Christian and particularly for a Catholic, given that, is it proper to say in a secular society that same-sex marriage is impossible?' I don't think it is.

STEVE CHALKE, Baptist minister and Christian social activist[2]

I wrote an article called 'A matter of integrity' recently because last year I conducted a blessing service for two good friends of mine who are part of the church that I lead here in central London. They were getting a civil partnership on the Friday and we did their blessing service on the Saturday. It was a celebration for the whole church community because a civil partnership is just that, a piece of legal apparatus, devoid of any social, spiritual content. And as a church community we wanted to stand with our friends, support them and encourage them into a lifelong faithful monogamous relationship just as we would do for a heterosexual couple.

I believe that the church has found itself in a really difficult position over the issue of gay marriage. I thought what John Gummer said was great but he typified the difficulty because he talked about secular marriage and, on the other hand, he said Catholics have a different view of marriage based on Christ, not the state. I think he's misread the Old and New Testament.

There were 1,500 years of perfectly good church history and theology that assumed the earth was flat and the earth was the centre of the universe. Copernicus overturned it and the Pope didn't like it and Martin Luther didn't like it, but it turned out Copernicus and Galileo were right. In actual fact I think that the ongoing task of theology is to read the Bible ever more closely. The point is this, the church is always going to be wrong-footed over the issue of gay marriage unless it sorts out a deeper and

[2] Steve Chalke founded Oasis UK in 1985 and Faithworks in 2001 to develop and campaign for faith-based welfare action as a way of transforming communities. He also leads Oasis Community Learning, a Multi-Academy Educational Trust which has so far set up 36 academies.

more profound issue: it's the issue of how it handles inclusion, and in this case particularly inclusion of gay people.

I've a friend who's part of the church that I lead now. At the age of 13 he went to his church elders in an evangelical Baptist church and told them he thought he was gay. They took him to the pastor and the elders who proceeded to exorcise him, telling him that he had the demon of homosexuality in him. It obviously didn't work well because they continued to do that for five years. By the time he was 18 he was alcoholic and had little or no self-esteem, not because he was gay but because of a misunderstanding of biblical texts, which led to the condemning of that young man. Gay people often are thrown out of church membership, often are banned from communion, are definitely banned from leadership and are banned from leading children's work or youth work.

So the church needs to re-evaluate the more profound question about how it includes gay people and then it will be able to sort out its position over gay marriage.

TINA BEATTIE, Professor of Theology at the University of Roehampton[3]

Let me begin with two brief observations. First, compulsory heterosexuality has perhaps been the biggest failed experiment in social engineering in human history. Second, I've been very struck how, in the debate about same-sex marriage, both those in favour and those against have an impossibly idealised understanding of what marriage is. We live in a culture where marriage is already broken in terms of the traditional Christian understanding of what it means. It's important to be realistic about the fact that even the very best marriage is probably more

---

[3] Tina Beattie is Director of the Digby Stuart Research Centre for Religion, Society and Human Flourishing at Roehampton University. She is a Roman Catholic theologian and her main areas of teaching and research are Christian theology and psychoanalysis, theologies and theories of gender, theology and the arts, and religion and human rights.

drudge than sexual romance if you're lucky and when you're young – and the worst marriage is a living hell on earth. If we come into this debate with a glossy idea of what marriage is, the burden on same-sex couples to live up to an impossible ideal to which no heterosexual couple would aspire becomes very great, and sets those marriages up to fail.

As a Roman Catholic myself I have enormous sympathy with almost everything that John Gummer says. I would argue that it's not for any religious minority to impose its views on the majority in a secular liberal democracy. Providing the process of legislation has been through public consultation and parliamentary debate, then Christians have a responsibility to accept the will of the people.

Where I disagree with John Gummer is that I don't think being a faithful Catholic means insisting that sacramental marriage is essentially heterosexual, without asking if there might not be an understanding of same-sex marriage that could be affirmed within faith communities, including churches.

By and large, Protestant debate tends to be around biblical prohibition of same-sex acts. It's important to recognise these are acts, not loving same-sex relationships. Also, the word 'homosexuality' is a nineteenth-century invention. So biblical scholars are not sure what kind of sex acts are actually being discussed and how far they can be applied to modernity anyway. The point of view that tends to inform the Catholic contribution to this debate is more informed by natural law and a heavy emphasis on procreation, and that too is open to debate.

All these debates have to be situated within the wider meaning and ethos of the gospel of Jesus Christ, which is primarily focused on incarnation and redemption. The doctrine of the incarnation – that Jesus Christ was fully human while remaining fully divine – puts the human body and materiality at the very centre of what it means to be a human made in the image of God. And sexuality is absolutely intrinsic to our bodiliness, whether we're celibate, sexually active, whatever.

So I would ask Christians who feel that they must oppose

same-sex marriage on what grounds it's legitimate to oppose a person who finds himself or herself attracted to persons of the same sex and who wants to express that sexuality through an aspiration to conform to the Christian ideal of a love that transcends the law and expresses itself through lifelong monogamous commitment for better or worse, in sickness and in health, till death us do part in the context of a same-sex rather than a heterosexual relationship. Far from undermining the Christian understanding of marriage I think this could be a very great gift and grace for our times, to call Christians back to a deeper appreciation of the kind of distinction that John Gummer makes between what can be the rather pared-down understanding of marriage that prevails under secular law, and the much richer, thicker description of marriage that can be derived from the Christian tradition.

JOHN MILBANK, Professor in Religion, Politics and Ethics at the University of Nottingham[4]

What most dispirits me about this entire issue is that something so important as marriage, something so primordial, something that precedes the foundation of the state, something that's both natural and religious, should have been treated so casually – as if it was not as important as something like tax reform. The Government has invented a consensus where there isn't one, it's ignored having a debate, it's written off large majorities. In relation to the gay issue there's a concern with minorities which is distorting the way we're thinking about majorities.

My next problem is that you can't really have equal marriage because sexual consummation can't be the criterion for gay marriage, nor can you use adultery as a ground for

[4] John Milbank is an Anglican theologian who directs the Centre for Theology and Philosophy at the University of Nottingham's Department of Theology and Religious Studies. He is a co-founder of the radical orthodoxy movement and the Chairman of the Res Publica think tank in London.

divorce. It would be monstrous to do these things. So therefore immediately and quite properly we are recognising that there is a certain difference in gay relationships, and this then begs the question of are we really giving them marriage at all, aren't we still retaining the difference between a civil partnership and marriage? If we were indeed to abolish the difference then I think the consequences are very worrying indeed, because at that point one would have removed the link between sex and procreation. Sexual difference would have become completely irrelevant, and the logical implication which a lot of lawyers have now spelt out is that your natural children – if you're a heterosexual couple – only become your children legally if the state allows you to adopt them.

This is why my opposition to gay marriage is of a radical kind. It's not in any sense of a conservative kind, and it's indeed shared with many gay people, especially gay people on the left. I think there was no demand for gay marriage, and I think the reason why it's been seized with such eagerness by the state is that it's weakening the basic mediating institution of marriage, it's allowing a direct relationship between the state and the market and children to creep in, and by weakening the link between sex and procreation you can go further down the road of technologising and politicising the population.

I think that the sexes have different and complementary points of view. For all of human history we've seen that it's fundamental to human social bonding to bring those complementary viewpoints together. We've also seen that it's crucial that there is a natural link between the sexual act and the bringing to birth of children. This is what binds our nature and culture together in the most fundamental way. If you sunder this link you reduce us to bare animality, on the one hand, and to mere rational control which will be handed over to the state, on the other hand.

This is why allowing same-sex marriage is such an anti-democratic measure. No longer can people understand their biological identity as emerging from a human interpersonal identity, an act of sexual love, even if it's a one-night stand. You would also undermine the whole logic of Christian mysticism and Christian doctrine by getting rid of the idea that the sexual partnership mirrors the partnership between Christ the bridegroom and the church as bride, and therefore you would undermine the logic of the understanding between God and creation where God has willed sexual difference. To admit gay marriage in the church would be to undo Christian doctrine.

STEPHEN HOLMES, Senior Lecturer in Systematic Theology at the University of St Andrews[5]

I'm afraid I want to start by doing some boring academic work of saying 'it depends what you mean' with almost every word in this question.

It depends what you mean by same-sex marriage. It seems to me entirely plausible to say, 'I am in favour of same-sex marriage as an ideal, but when I look at the bill on the table in Westminster, or the different bill on the table in Holyrood, I find myself unable to support the particular way it's being worked out in these contexts.' And so we need to know, are we asking about an intellectual ideal or are we asking about a particular policy proposal? If we're in favour of the intellectual ideal, is it actually achievable in policy terms? In English law there are serious problems when introducing genuinely equal marriage that have not been faced up to.

Second, what do we mean by 'oppose'? It's a very binary word and Linda's presented to us a survey where people have been asked, 'Do you oppose?' Does this mean I am rabidly against? Does it mean I have minor preferences in these directions? These

---

[5] Dr Stephen Holmes lectures on historical and systematic theology and homiletics. He is a Baptist and has a special interest in evangelical Christianity. He has published books on a range of central themes in theology, as well as Baptist tradition and practice, and Puritan history.

are the sorts of things that a survey cannot indicate to you. And this concerns me because this issue is being played out in our national media as the central issue of interest for the churches in Britain today. And it just isn't. I suspect that if you went round the churches that I know and serve, and asked, 'Would you rather the Government dropped its proposals for same-sex marriage or the regressive welfare cuts that were introduced a couple of weeks ago?', there would be a fairly unanimous answer and it wouldn't be about same-sex marriage.

Third, what do we mean by Christians? Linda's already indicated to us that the numbers even in the very blunt instrument of the survey that she presented show that when you switch from people who say they identify with the tradition to people who are active participants in the tradition then you find the mood shifting. A sociologist I respect very greatly wrote in the *Guardian* on 5 December last year a powerful piece as to why, when questions that matter and that have fuzzy edges are on the table, we should be very concerned about opinion polls. I thought it was an excellent piece Linda: I'm grateful that you wrote it!

On the point, 'What do we mean by Christian?' we have focused entirely on UK Christians. Churches are not nationally bounded organisations. They do not have the luxury of a kind of moral parochialism that national governments have. We're told that the average Christian in the world today is a 19-year-old woman in Chad or Nigeria. If we took the same survey questions to her I think we could be very confident what her responses would be. In Chad and North Nigeria there is not a very significant movement in favour of same-sex marriage.

So do Christians oppose same-sex marriage? I think with a good definition of Christian the answer is probably yes, they very certainly oppose same-sex marriage if it was suggested to take place in their churches. I think you'd find more division on the question of same-sex marriage in the wider society, but it would be genuine and serious division.

DISCUSSION

Children and procreation

Charles Clarke I'm going to kick off with the children and procreation issue. Could you just talk a little bit about how important it is in the views that you've expressed that one has to take account of who's bringing up children, whether a same-sex couple could bring up children, and if so how that could operate? Is it philosophical or practical views which inform your thinking?

Tina Beattie Back to my theme of idealisation. I could perhaps be pushed to say that in an ideal world a wonderful woman and a wonderful man who love each other deeply would have wonderful children in a hunky-dory family and that would probably be a very good thing for children. But Christianity is not about an idealised world, it's about the broken world that we actually live in and its failings and sins and struggles. In Britain today there are somewhere between 75,000 and 100,000 children in care. Camila Batmanghelidjh estimates that probably double that number should be in care. Children are the most vulnerable members of our society today and that has nothing to do with the consequences of same-sex relationships. It's because of the breakdown of heterosexual relationships.

John Milbank I'm not against gay adoption. I think it's a second best. I probably would slightly more emphasise the need ideally for a mother and a father, but I think that to be brought up by a loving gay couple can be way better than languishing in some not very good children's home.

But that for me is not the real issue. The question is the relationship of sex to having children, that's the nub of the issue and that's where there is an ineradicable natural difference. We have marriage historically for heterosexuals not homosexuals, despite the fact that homosexuality is a phenomenon in many societies. The point is that it's this natural act of sex that leads naturally to children and therefore is absolutely crucial in the continuation of the human race, the link between our animality and our sociality, the setting up of kinship patterns that are absolutely fundamental.

Steve Chalke Procreation is a benefit of marriage for some people but not for all. We promote marriage for older couples, widowers and widows getting married. Marriage isn't about procreation for these people, it's about companionship and it's about hope.

On the point about adoption and bringing up children, I'm responsible for 28 schools; Oasis has 20,000 young people in our schools in England. I can tell you this, that the problem with the development and growth of young people today is not that they happen to be brought up by a gay couple. It's the dad who's never there, who doesn't care, who beats the mum up; it's the mum that's absorbed in her own interests who never reads to the child. The couple that I did a blessing service for, I respect them, I love them, they're culturally engaged, they're intelligent, they're giving, they're caring. If they reach the place where they wanted to adopt a child I would support that wholly, both for them and for the child involved. I believe it would be a wonderful home.

Stephen Holmes I think we need to distinguish very clearly between an institution and the activities or intentions of those entering it. A university is an institution that's devoted to research, to education. People will come to university because they want to play in a sports team or start a political career, or all sorts of things, but that doesn't change the nature of the institution. The goods of Christian marriage have traditionally been identified as three: it images the relationship of Christ to the church, it provides faithful companionship and friendship, and it is the place where children are brought into the world.

To suddenly say we can have an account of marriage which can only possibly account for two of those goods is not impossible but it needs to be argued. We need to examine how those goods are founded, how they belong together. It occurs to me as a thought experiment, that if you had a proposal for same-sex marriage that included within it an ineradicable intention to adopt, then it might be more acceptable to the churches. In society, as opposed to in the church, marriage has been an institution that has been oriented around the begetting and bringing up of children. The point is that the societal institution of marriage has been in civil law a place where children are brought into the world, given their place in society.

The pace of change

Charles Clarke John, you made in your presentation the charge that essentially this was all being dealt with too casually, not seriously enough, rushed through. I now want to ask the panel whether you think that's a fair charge.

Steve Chalke I don't agree with John, I think it is being thought through. I think that everything starts as a mess; I think that debate draws out truth. I've taken part in more than one committee across the road in Parliament about this and I've been astonished by what I've learnt through the debate and the discussion, and the depth and complexity these conversations have gone into. I think we're part way through a process. I'm glad that the bill comes before Parliament because I think that that is the way that you deal with these issues in a democracy. Society is a debate and we find truth together. I'm glad of the debate but I don't think it's being rushed.

Stephen Holmes I do think it's being rushed. I think there's good evidence for this in partisan pronouncements from both sides of the debate. One of the things you find on both sides is an appeal to the experience of countries that have introduced same-sex marriage. Both sides of the debate have got their favourite countries. One can say it happened ten years ago here and, look, the number of marriages has fallen off, the number of children going into care has shot up, it's clearly been a disaster. And then on the other side they say, look, it happened 12 years ago here and there's been no effect on society at all. The data being cited is correct but what it shows you is that we don't know. So it seems to me that the question of whether the extension of marriage to same-sex couples is a good thing or a bad thing for society is still a very open question, and I think knowing the answer to that question before you do it is worthwhile.

Tina Beattie   I'm sympathetic to John's argument that it has been rushed through rather willy-nilly (if that's not an unfortunate expression)! The debate was pushed forward, but now that it's been put on the table, I'm sympathetic to the argument that we should go ahead and have the debate. If we refused to consider changes in law and public policy on these intimate and important areas of people's lives until we could be sure they would be good for society, we'd never change anything. Everything we do has the potential for good or for bad, and every considered and well-intentioned change brings unexpected consequences, some of which will be beneficial and some harmful. I think I am glad the debate has happened. But I'm very cynical about why a government that is doing so much else to destroy family life in terms of economic policies and social welfare is so eager to promote different forms of marriage and the family in this one particular issue.

John Milbank   I don't think it's a matter of looking at the evidence or trying to make calculations. It's rather saying, 'What does this actually mean in terms of what marriage is and has been historically and conceptually?' And I think that's the debate that hasn't happened. It's irrelevant to say old people marry for companionship. Marriage is about sexual difference and about the link of sex to procreation.

Inclusion

Charles Clarke   Steve made a general argument that the issue of same-sex marriage is a subset of the broader issue that there ought to be greater inclusion of gay people in the churches. Do you agree?

Linda Woodhead   In our poll we also asked people whether they think the churches are welcoming to gay people. Among 18–24-year-olds, only 17% think that churches are welcoming to gay people. So whatever the churches say, or are, that's the perception.

Stephen Holmes   I think Steve's point that churches have been unwelcoming is a very important one. If there is one person in the country who does not feel welcome in a Christian church then the church is doing something wrong. So it seems to me that the issue is inclusion of all people.

Tina Beattie   I think that's right, but there are such hugely complex questions about psychology and social relationships here as well. Inclusion is about allowing people to be who they honestly are and finding acceptance, and all of us have different boundaries around that. The Anglican and Catholic Churches probably have, anecdotally, a relatively high proportion of gay Christians within them. But what do you do with a totally inclusive church where everyone can out themselves overnight in cultures that are constructed around not doing that? Yes, that would be a wonderful thing, but I would like to be at the breakfast table in the Vatican the day after that happens. I think chaos would reign for a little while. Eventually, I suppose, the great dream would be for it not to matter how a person is sexually defined when they come into a church or any other space. We're people, and why should gay people feel that the one thing that identifies them in a community is gayness? Of course that's true of any marginalised excluded minority, but oh for the day when it's not true of sexual minorities – or of any other minority either.

John Milbank   I think I fundamentally agree with Tina that the real point is not to put people into categories. It's part of my reasoning about gay relationships. By the way, I am in favour of the blessing of gay relationships in church, I just feel that that needs to be distinguished from marriage. Part of my reasoning here is that it's wrong to say to gay people, 'Well, what kind of physical acts if any does your very close love and friendship involve?' If there is a reason for doing that with heterosexual people, there is absolutely none in relation to homosexual people. That's a matter for them and their confessor.

Steve Chalke   Coming out is still against the law of the church and coming out is a really dangerous thing for anyone to do. The way that the churches have treated gay people is a scandal. It is appalling. The record is absolutely awful. I sat talking to someone, a friend of mine who runs trains in this country, a day or two ago and I asked him how many gay young men had thrown themselves under his trains. He said there's no research that explains why young men throw themselves under our trains. Didn't deny it happened. I said, talk to the Samaritans. That's the reality.

Speaking from experience

Adam Dinham   I'm Professor of Faith and Public Policy at Goldsmiths, University of London. I've got a question and some points I'd like to challenge you with, John. You say, I think, that same-sex marriage goes against God's will and that it reduces us to, I think the phrase you used was 'bare animality', and I think it's an unfortunate way of putting it but I understood the argument. You also say that gay marriage can't be real marriage because it can't be consummated, and I think you're probably referring, are you, to the drafting of the same-sex marriage bill?

John Milbank   I'm referring to a well-known fact of life.

Adam Dinham   It's a good job this is a debate. The drafters of the same-sex marriage bill of course can't come up with an operational definition of consummation. And I think that reflects their homophobia, not whether or not I consummated my marriage. I'm in a civil partnership, with a Muslim as it happens, and I assure you we consummated our marriage and it feels quite natural to us.

You also talked, several of you on the panel, about this being rushed through as a debate. I'm 39 and for me it's been a lifetime, and worse for lots of people much older.

John, you said that marriage is primordial and it seems to me that homosexuality is primordial too, and I wonder what you'd say to that.

John Milbank   I'm not wanting to deny at all that you've consummated your civil partnership. What I'm objecting to is the idea that that could readily be defined in the case of homosexuals. It's only in the case of heterosexuality that there is a clear definition of consummation because it's a sexual act that can lead to procreation. That's exactly why they're being the reverse of homophobic in taking that into account. On the contrary, they're respecting difference. It's all the time this issue of difference. I'm not denying that there's homosexuality in the animal kingdom, it's certainly always been present in the human kingdom; there are African tribes where you have to go through a homosexual phase, or ancient Athens. Nonetheless it never crossed their minds that this would be considered marriage, and we at least have to ask why not.

Tina Beattie   If you look at the Catholic theology of marriage since it became a sacrament in the Middle Ages it's a muddle, because nobody has ever established whether it's the intention of the couple during the ceremony that makes the sacrament, or consummation. So there's a blurry area anyway. This emphasis on consummation as a biological sex act of the sort that any dog in the street can participate in seems to me utterly reductive. The sacrament of marriage is primarily the relationship between Christ and the church, and if you think that can only mean sexual penetration of a woman by a man then the nuptial theology of the body you like so much falls down. The sacrament of marriage between Christ and the church has nothing to do with the kind of biological literalism you're talking about.

Steve Chalke The Catholic Church has seven sacraments and marriage is one of them. The Protestant Churches have two sacraments, which are simply communion (the Eucharist) and baptism. The definition of marriage, well perhaps the definition I'm working with, is I believe that we are made for intimacy. I believe that that reflects who God is; even God is a community, Father, Son and Holy Spirit. I am most human when I am in community; I am most human when I can enjoy the intimacy of relationship. I think it's an awful crime, an injustice, that we banished people to live lives of loneliness and sometimes lives of deception. I think that we need to find a place within the church where people in a same sex-relationship can celebrate that.

This *is* an issue of justice and it's about time churches woke up to understand that. And too many people live lives of depression and mental illness and rejection around the world because we don't take this issue of justice seriously. And to the girl who's 19, I think you said Steve, who's living in a Nigerian village, actually in Nigeria and Uganda where I work as Oasis this is a real issue. And that girl might be 19 and lesbian but can't say it for fear of death. So this is a justice issue and it's about time we dealt with it as such.

Stephen Holmes I take entirely your point about homophobia in Africa. I have no argument with any of that.

The question is whether a society needs to introduce same-sex marriage as opposed to a practice of civil partnership. Whether that is a question of human rights or justice has been extensively tested before the European Court of Human Rights and they have said no.

SOME MEDIA REACTION

Given that the churches have really pulled out the big guns and made this the big issue that they are going to stand on, it is surprising that not even half of active churchgoers are opposed.

Linda Woodhead, quoted by John Bingham in the *Daily Telegraph*,
17 April 2013

Overall, all those who identified with a religion were evenly split on allowing same-sex couples to marry, with 43% for and 43% against.

Christianity Today, quoting the YouGov survey findings, 17 April 2013

The section of religious people most opposed to same-sex marriage is made up of those who both believe in God with certainty and make decisions primarily on the basis of explicit religious sources – God, scriptures, teachings and religious leaders.

National Secular Society Newsletter,
quoting the YouGov survey findings, 19 April 2013

Summary: WHAT HAVE WE LEARNED? by LINDA WOODHEAD

● The single most important thing we learned from this debate and the poll which informed it is that a majority of Christians in Great Britain are in favour of allowing same-sex marriage, and that religious people as a whole are evenly split on the issue. This finding was widely reported in the national media because it was not known before. Previously it had been widely assumed that Christians were opposed to the legislation which is currently working its way through Parliament.

- One reason why this false assumption had gained ground is that church leaders, including the leaders of the Anglican and Catholic Churches in this country, are strongly opposed to the change. Another is that many people see religion as a conservative force. Our poll and debate teaches us that by no means all religious people are conservative, and that what religious leaders say does not necessarily reflect the views of their 'followers'.

- The survey was also illuminating about the reasons people take a stand either for or against gay marriage. It showed that those who are in favour of allowing same-sex marriage – both religious and non-religious – are particularly influenced by their commitment to the principle of equality. Presumably they feel that it is unfair to treat people differently on the basis of their sexuality, and to deny them a privilege which heterosexuals enjoy. On the other side of the debate, those who are opposed to the introduction of same-sex marriage ground their opposition in a belief that men and women are *so* significantly different from one another that if you allow two people of the same sex to marry, it is not really 'marriage', which can only be between a man and a woman.

- The debate between our panellists revealed that Christians draw on these same arguments, but appeal to other considerations as well. John Milbank is opposed to any form of same-sex marriage, and Stephen Holmes is opposed to the current legislation and would like more time for the issue to be resolved. Both appeal to the argument that there is something irreducible about the bond between a man and a woman, and Milbank makes this point particularly forcefully, arguing that the ability of a man and a woman to consummate their marriage through male penetration of the woman, and thereby to procreate, is what makes marriage exclusive to heterosexual couples. He believes that such marriage is foundational to society, culture and true religion, and that redefining it will undermine them all.

- As a Catholic, John Gummer accepts his church's teaching that marriage is a lifelong sacramental bond between a man and a woman, but he does not believe that it is right for the churches to impose this view on the rest of society. As a member of the House of Lords, he will therefore vote in favour of the legislation. Steve Chalke does not say whether he approves of the current legislation or not, because he believes that the more important issue for Christians is that the churches become places which are welcoming and inclusive to gay and lesbian people.

● Tina Beattie is the strongest and most straightforward supporter of same-sex marriage on our panel, and she defends it on Christian theological grounds. She thinks that it is crude to narrow marriage down to procreative sex, and prefers to think of it in terms of a bond of embodied love. She points out that love and embodiment are at the very heart of the Christian gospel. Since same-sex couples can obviously have as strong a bond of love as deeply as other couples, allowing them to partake of the sacrament of marriage will enlarge and enrich our understanding of marriage.

● Whatever their views, all our speakers acknowledge the prejudice and hurt which gay and lesbian people have suffered in the past, and deplore this. Some think that allowing same-sex marriage is important in changing the situation, while the others disagree and worry that the change will damage society as a whole.

DISCUSSION QUESTIONS

1. What makes a marriage? Is it the commitment partners make to each other, the legal contract, recognition by others, God's blessing, the sexual act of consummation or something else?
2. If marriage is a bond between a man and a woman, how can it include same-sex relationships without ceasing to be marriage?
3. Why do same-sex couples want to be married? Why might they think that civil partnership is not as good?
4. Our poll shows that every generation is more in favour of same-sex marriage than the one that went before. Why do you think this change has taken place?
5. Do you agree with Lord Deben that state marriage should be separated from Christian marriage?

6. Just 21% of survey respondents thought that churches are welcoming to gay, lesbian and bisexual people. What do you think, and do you think that can change?

RESOURCES

View the debate at www.faithdebates.org.uk.

Read the Church of England's statement on 'Same-sex Marriage and the Church of England'.

The Lesbian and Gay Christian Movement represents the interests of lesbian and gay Christians, and the website includes a Resources section.

Steve Chalke's statement, 'A matter of integrity: the church, sexuality, inclusion and an open conversation' is available at http://www.oasisuk.org/article.aspx?menuId=31887.

CHAPTER SIX
Should we legislate to permit assisted dying?

People in the context of a terminal illness should have
the right to choose how they die ... it's their right and I
think we're not compassionate as a society if our law
doesn't change to catch up with the practice.

Charles Falconer

I'm afraid as a clinician I can tell you we can't really define
who is terminally ill. Most conditions in medicine are
incurable, most conditions in medicine are progressive,
and we don't know how rapidly they're going to progress.

Ilora Finlay

If doctors are involved it becomes a duty of care. So
that's why introducing something like this is a change in
climate, it is a game-changer.

Rob George

People often say they don't want to be a burden to
their families. Well, I bloody well do want to be a burden
to my family, and actually I want my family to be a
burden to me, and that seems to me to be entirely what
it is to be in a family and in a community.

Giles Fraser

Opening comment by **CHARLES CLARKE**

This profound debate is often confused by language. As pointed out
below, 'assisted dying' refers to circumstances when someone helps
another person to end their own life intentionally and voluntarily, usually

because they have a terminal illness. For example, this may mean providing the means, such as drugs or equipment, which are necessary. The people providing such help might be medical professionals.

Suicide itself ceased to be a criminal offence in Britain in 1961. The contemporary debate has been provoked by a number of sad cases where some individuals, living in painful and tragic circumstances, have sought to end their lives and, unable to do so physically, have asked others to help them. But help could only be offered at risk of criminal conviction. A bill to legalise assistance in such cases has been presented to Parliament by Lord Falconer, who participated in this debate.

The opinion polling for this debate showed that the majority of people, including those with religious beliefs, support such a change. However, at the moment, most MPs do not. Some people have profound objections to such legislation on the grounds that any extinction of human life should be illegal.

A wider range of concerns arise around the boundaries of such action. Should assistance only be legal in cases of terminal illness, and how can this be defined with any certainty? How can anyone be certain that the individual genuinely wants to choose death and that they are of 'right mind'? Is the selfless desire to remove oneself as a burden to others legitimate? Might someone be pressurised even by close family for good reasons (to end suffering) or bad (to inherit money earlier)? And, are the professional guidelines for medical professionals sufficient to guide their actions, or is clear law also needed?

And, apart from the individual circumstances of particular cases, would such legislation in some sense cheapen and undervalue life itself? Is not suffering part of the human condition and is it right to reduce it, or surrender to it?

These issues are eternal, but attitudes are changing, and the reasons for that are interesting. The poll which supports this debate shows that one is that so many people feel that they have a right to decide what to do with their own life. It is also less common to believe that suffering is a value in its own right, or has some larger religious purpose. Perhaps the relation between 'patients' and medical 'experts' has also changed quite profoundly. Whatever the reason, there is now a major discrepancy between where the law is and where public opinion has ended up.

Setting the scene – by **LINDA WOODHEAD**

The debate about whether we should legislate to permit assisted dying is proceeding so rapidly, and is so heated, that even the terms we use are contested. So to make for clarity of discussion, it's useful to clarify some key terms on the table at the outset.

'Euthanasia' is the most traditional one. It literally means a 'good death', so it is a very broad notion. 'Assisted suicide' means helping someone to commit suicide for whatever reason they might want to do that. 'Assisted dying' is narrower, because it implies that the person has a terminal illness and is in the process of dying anyway, so assisting them to die is helping them in the context of imminent death. Sometimes people also want to add the word 'voluntary' to these terms – obviously if they're involuntary they amount to murder. A further distinction which is sometimes drawn is between physician-assisted forms of euthanasia, and those in which no physician takes part.

The plethora of terms reflects the complexity of the debate. If people say they are in favour of allowing euthanasia they may perhaps mean physician-assisted dying, or non-physician-assisted suicide, or something different again. So there is no standard survey question you can use to gauge people's views.

Most of the questions we used in the YouGov poll referred to throughout these debates we designed ourselves, but in this case we decided to use a standard question which YouGov have run before: 'Do you think British law should be kept as it is, or should it be changed so that people with incurable diseases have the right to ask close friends or relatives to help them commit suicide, without those friends or relatives risking prosecution?' When defined in this way, it turns out that a large majority of people (70%) want the law to be changed, 16% to stay as it is, and 14% don't know. So there is strong public support for a change in the law.

Most surprising was how many religious people agree – 64% support a change in the law, 21% think it should stay as it is, and 14% don't know. Figure 1 (see p.134) shows the variation between those who identify with different religious traditions.

Support for change is extremely high among Anglicans – at 72% it is actually higher than the support among the general public. A significant margin of Catholics are also in favour – 56% in favour, 30% against. As in relation to some other issues we have looked at in this series, Muslims and Baptists are the exceptions; they do not think that assisted dying should be allowed.

Our survey shows that there is even a high level of support for a change in the law among religious people who actively practise their faith within a group. Among churchgoing Anglicans, 59% support assisted dying, and a quarter oppose it. Catholics are fairly evenly split for and against. Muslims are very strongly opposed (Figure 2, see p.134).

On this issue, as on many of the others discussed in this book, it is clear that the official teachings of many religions and their leaders are not shared by a very significant proportion of their 'followers'.

We also asked people about their reasons for supporting or opposing assisted dying. A massive 82% of those in favour cited as a reason that 'an individual has the right to choose when and how to die' (Figure 3, see p.135). Among those who opposed a change in the law, there is less consensus. Interestingly, the reason that religious campaigners against euthanasia often cite – that human life is sacred ('the sanctity of life') – only came fourth in the list of reasons. The most-cited reason among those who oppose change is that if assisted dying is allowed, vulnerable people could be, or feel, pressurised to die (Figure 4, see p.135).

It's important to remember that our survey asked a very particular question about non-physician-assisted dying. Different questions elicit different responses. For example, a British Social Attitudes survey in 2005 asked a question about the right to die of a person with a painful and incurable disease from which they will not die, for example severe arthritis, and in this case just 13% thought that physician-assisted suicide should be allowed. So it seems that the strong support is for assisted dying, but not necessarily for other forms of assisted suicide.

'Euthanasia is the termination of a person's life, in order to end suffering. Do you think British law should be kept as it is, or should it be changed so that people with incurable diseases have the right to ask close friends or relatives to help them commit suicide, without those friends or relatives risking prosecution?'

	None	Anglican	Roman Catholic	Presbyterian	Methodist	Baptist	Jewish	Hindu	Muslim	Sikh
Support change	81	72	56	61	62	43	69	36	26	69
Oppose change	9	15	30	24	23	45	21	28	55	14
Don't know	10	13	14	15	15	12	10	36	19	17

Figure 1: Religious adherents. YouGov for Westminster Faith Debates 2013.

	Anglican	Roman Catholic	Church of Scotland	Methodist/Baptist	Pentacostal	Jewish	Hindu	Muslim	Sikh
Support change	59	44	45	49	6	64	47	23	73
Oppose change	25	42	40	40	78	25	36	63	11
Don't	16	14	15	11	16	11	17	14	17

Figure 2: People who actively participate in a church or other religious group. YouGov for Westminster Faith Debates 2013.

'You said that you think the current law on euthanasia should be changed to allow assisted suicide in some circumstances. Which of the following best describes your view? Please tick all that apply.'

An individual has the right to choose when and how to die	82
It is preferable to drawn-out suffering	77
Those assisting suiside should not fear prosecution	76
It's happening anyway and regulation would improve safety and delivery	51
The national health and welfare systems cannot provide decent end-of-life care	35
Other/Don't know	2

Figure 3: YouGov for Westminster Faith Debates 2013.

'You said that you think the current law on euthanasia should be kept as it is. Which of the following best describes your view? Please tick all that apply.'

Vunerable people could be, or feel, pressured to die	59
You can never build in enough safeguards	48
Human life is sacred	48
Death should take its natural course	48
No one can ever be certain that they really want to die, but the decision is irreversible	43
Other/Don't know	6

Figure 4: YouGov for Westminster Faith Debates 2013.

Of all the issues we have discussed in these debates, this is the one on which there is the greatest divergence between popular opinion and current legislation. Lord Charles Falconer, one of our speakers, has been active in trying to close that gap, and is currently proposing a change in the law. But a recent ComRes survey found that a majority of MPs are still opposed to such change.

THE DEBATE

CHARLES FALCONER, Member of the House of Lords[1]

I support legislating to allow assisted dying. In my book, that means assisting somebody to take their own life but in the context of a terminal illness. I am motivated to support this by my experience of seeing how people die and listening to people explaining what their experience of the death of a loved one has been. If you are ill, if that illness is almost certainly going to lead to your death, should you fight for every minute, should you be forced to keep on going when society has said we don't outlaw suicide?

We as a society should normally do our best to stop people trying to commit suicide, but where your life is about to end, and where you fear the loss of control, or maybe the life that you are leading is absolutely awful, is it wrong to have a situation where a doctor can give you a prescription that will allow you to take your own life? In my view it is not. It is the compassionate and right thing to do, and in a way society has reached that conclusion on its own.

We have a law at the moment that says it's a criminal offence to assist somebody else to kill themselves, and the maximum sentence for such a crime is 14 years. But what the police and the prosecutors are constantly faced with is people who, with the best possible motive, because they feel compassion towards those that they love and who are dying, assist them to take their own life.

The most common way that's happening at the moment is that people go to Switzerland where it's lawful to take your own life. Friends and relatives help them by taking them to the airport, accompanying them when they go. The prosecuting authorities know that's a crime, it's assisting somebody to kill themselves, but they just do not have the stomach to prosecute them because

[1] Charles Falconer is a Labour peer who held a number of ministerial posts in the Labour Government in the period 1997–2007, including Solicitor General and Lord Chancellor. He chaired the Commission on Assisted Dying whose final report was published in January 2012.

they believe people here are acting with compassion, helping somebody in the context of a very, very difficult situation. So the Director of Public Prosecutions has issued guidelines which say, in effect, I won't prosecute people if they're motivated by compassion. But these guidelines make it clear that he would prosecute a doctor if he assisted somebody to commit suicide.

So you have this ridiculous hypocritical law which says amateur assistance in this country is allowed but professional assistance is not. It is a ridiculous denial of the facts. Can you introduce a law or do you have to depend upon the discretion of the Director of Public Prosecutions? I think you can introduce a law that says two doctors have got to be satisfied that you are terminally ill, you have a specified period of time to live in their opinion, and there's no reason why you shouldn't be assisted to die. It's happened in other countries. For example, in Oregon it's worked incredibly well without any damage to palliative care, indeed palliative care has improved.

I think it's time for us as a society to catch up in our law with what people are already doing. People in the context of a terminal illness should have the right to choose how they die. I don't think anybody should kill them; I think they've got to kill themselves, but it's their right, and I think we're not compassionate as a society if our law doesn't change to catch up with the practice.

ROB GEORGE, Professor of Palliative Care and clinician[2]

I was with patients this afternoon. I've come from work, that's what I do every day, look after people who are dying. Probably about 20,000 over the course of my professional career. The interesting thing is that if you ask society in general about their views, you

[2] Rob George is responsible at Guy's and St Thomas' Hospitals in London for community palliative and end-of-life care. He advises the Government and sits on various ethics committees. Previously he pioneered HIV and non-cancer palliative care at UCL Hospitals, and was involved with research projects at the Cicely Saunders Institute.

essentially get a report like the YouGov report Linda presented. But if you ask clinicians, the numbers are reversed. Why is that?

Seventy per cent of doctors are firmly against assisting suicide. I'm just going to deal with one principal reason, which is that we know how complex and difficult and subtle it is to manage somebody as they engage and struggle with the issues around death and dying.

I think that for many of us in society these situations are exceptionally difficult. It's what we call the burden of witness. An example from my personal life was when my father was dying from dementia and my mother said, 'I can't bear all of this suffering.' I said, 'Mother, why don't we just ask him?' So I asked him and he said, 'Don't be ridiculous, I'm not suffering at all.' So I said, 'Mum, he's just said he's not suffering.' She said, 'Yes, but I just can't bear seeing all this suffering.' She was speaking about herself.

Managing suffering is what the human condition is about, and that's what society is about, helping people to transcend difficult situations. There are many people in society who have dreadful disabilities and all sorts of challenges who do transcend, and I wish we would find out more about how they deal with it and how we can help people who can't cope, because we will never take suffering away.

The problem is that if doctors are involved in bringing life to an end, you've effectively reclassified ending a life – killing, to be blunt – as being a potential good. And once that happens you've changed its category in society, you've turned it from a freedom to kill yourself into an entitlement to be killed.

Do you know there's no difference morally between giving someone a prescription for antibiotics and injecting them with intravenous antibiotics? The moral decision is they needed antibiotics. So this idea that somehow there's a difference between assisted dying or assisted suicide is, I think, a confused position. If doctors are involved it becomes a duty of care. So that's why introducing something like this is a change in climate, it is a game-changer.

The final point I want to make is that I think there is an absolute moral reason why this is wrong. I believe it is wrong fundamentally to require somebody else to kill you in your own best interests. Why? Because it is a moral hazard to you, the person doing it, and I do not have an entitlement under any moral code to say you are required to do that because I want you to.

What's worse? Is it not to kill people who might want to die or to kill people who might want to live? Because once society allows killing people who want to die, it will then change the ambient culture and start to introduce obligations and duties on others to make that possible, and in fact the data from Oregon demonstrates that. There's something like a fivefold rise of people saying they want their life ended because they consider themselves to be a burden on the family. Whether this idea that they are a burden is real or perceived is irrelevant, it has become an increasing reason why people feel that they ought or they want to have their life ended.

GILES FRASER, *Guardian* columnist and Anglican priest[3]

People often say they don't want to be a burden to their families. Well, I bloody well do want to be a burden to my family, and actually I want my family to be a burden to me, and that seems to me to be entirely what it is to be in a family and in a community.

My problem with the way in which this debate is framed is not the conclusion. I think probably Charlie Falconer will have his way. The opinion poll seemed to go that way and I suspect that'll happen, and I'm not going to beat myself up and think that's the worst thing in the world. But there is a broader issue here which really does concern me, about the way in which the sort of individualism that we have in our society is now

[3] Giles Fraser is priest-in-charge of St Mary's, Newington, and a columnist and broadcaster. He featured prominently in the news in 2011 when Occupy London set up camp at St Paul's Cathedral, where he held the post of Canon Chancellor. He resigned in opposition to the Cathedral authorities' plans to use force to evict the protesters.

beginning to infect even the way that we think about death.

If you ask people how they want to die, the majority of people will say they want to die painlessly, quickly, in their sleep without being a bother, without being a burden to other people. They almost want to die without knowing they're dying or without anybody else knowing they're dying. Dying is so much less a public phenomenon now than it used to be, but in 100 years' time everybody in this room will be food for daffodils.

The important thing about recognising death and recognising our vulnerability is that it's an absolute part of what makes us human. That acceptance of our suffering, of our loss, of our vulnerability, is a crucial part of how we care for each other.

This business about an individual has the right to choose – I think the origins of that are probably in market capitalism, and it's an ethics which originates in probably something as fundamentally inane as choosing cornflakes in a supermarket. I have to choose, I have a right to choose, choice is the ultimate moral value. I think that's fundamentally rooted in the way in which capitalism has changed our moral values.

I want to talk not about the individual's right to choose, I want to talk about communities and the way in which communities look after each other. And so for me things like the right to choose, self-determination, yes, even things like suffering, are not the trump card. There's a really great question that the philosopher Martha Nussbaum asks: 'Why do gods in ancient Greek literature fall in love with human beings?' Gods are perfect, they can never die, nothing ever goes wrong with them, they're absolutely completely pristine. Why would gods fall in love with messy, vulnerable human beings that decay and produce waste and fail and things like that? Because there's so much about human beings and why we're important that's bound up with our vulnerabilities. Courage, love, care for others – that is not done in a world where everybody's immune from pain and loss.

I think the way in which we try and anaesthetise ourselves from pain and loss and suffering ultimately has a detrimental effect on our relationships with each other. You're feeling a bit miserable. Take a pill for that. It takes off the highs but it takes off the lows. All we're trying to do is anaesthetise our suffering and actually I think one of the problems from that is we limit ourselves from each other. Yes, I want to be a burden to my family, and I want them to be a burden on me, and I want to care for them and I hope they care for me.

ILORA FINLAY, Member of the House of Lords and Honorary Professor of Palliative Medicine at Cardiff University[4]

The problem that we're facing here is that what you, Charlie, want to do is to license doctors to prescribe lethal overdoses for their patients, in effect, on request. You talk about safeguards and you say that the law currently isn't working. I would like to challenge both of those presumptions.

Firstly, is the law working? There's clear guidance over prosecution that's been developed by Keir Starmer (Director of Public Prosecutions), and there has been no argument about those who have not been prosecuted. Why? Because we have laws which are there to protect people in society who are vulnerable. When those laws are broken our framework allows us to interpret compassionately what has happened – what is the evidence, is there a danger to society? – and it will prosecute if there is. But if not, there is no prosecution. But we do not change the law ahead of an event. Take a mother who steals because her children are hungry. We would not expect that mother to be prosecuted. We would expect the DPP to look at this and look compassionately on the situation.

What about safeguards? If you look at Oregon, which some

[4] Baroness Finlay is actively involved in debates on health issues and has served on the Select Committee on the Assisted Dying for the Terminally Ill Bill. She has developed palliative and hospice services across Wales. She has worked with Marie Curie Cancer Care since 1987 and is now a National Vice President. She remains an active clinician, teacher and academic as well as her involvement in Parliament.

claim is working and has safeguards, there has been a steady rise in the number of assisted suicides and requests for assisted suicide since they changed their law. At the moment we have about 20 people a year who will go to Switzerland. But if you go on those Oregon figures you'd be talking about 1,200 people a year, relative to our population.

You talk about people being terminally ill. Well, I'm afraid as a clinician I can tell you we can't really define who is terminally ill. Most conditions in medicine are incurable, most conditions in medicine are progressive, and we don't know how rapidly they're going to progress. The margin of error extends into months or years. Even if you think someone's in the last 48 hours of life you only have about a 97% probability of being right. Three per cent of the people you stop treating actually improve, because the treatment was doing more harm than the illness.

If you want to have an accurate diagnosis, I'm sorry, but medicine is not that good at it. The Royal College of Pathologists, in evidence to our select committee, told us about 1 in 20 people at post-mortem are found to have died from a condition that they were not being treated for. We do our best, but we don't always get it right.

As for prognosis, I've had many patients where I have really thought they were going to be dead in a very short space of time and I have been completely wrong. Sadly I've had many patients whom I thought would live for quite a time and I've also been wrong.

I've been struck at how patients, when they've achieved whatever it was they set themselves as their last goal in life, die, and die peacefully. But we don't hear about those. We hear about bad deaths, but you don't hear about good deaths. So it's understandable that a population out there is getting scared about a crisis in care that they're told about.

What about other safeguards you propose? You would say that people have to have capacity. Well, I'm afraid you can't assess capacity as a one-off event, you just can't do it. Even Oregon has shown that 1 in 6 of the people who were followed in depth and went on to end their lives with physician-assisted suicide actually had an untreated, undiagnosed depression.

What about coercion? Internal coercion: the sense that 'I don't want to be a burden, I don't want to be a financial drain on my family.' I think that internal pressure is increasing. But if you have doctors assisting people, there is also an external pressure, which is that if the doctor agrees to do this then I must be right that my life is not worth living because the doctor agrees that I would be better off dead.

Last of all, we don't live in a perfect world. While most parents love their children, not all children love their parents. There are pressures; people looking after someone get carer fatigue. They get worn out. That's normal. But I want health care to have to keep on striving to improve quality of life and to accept death as the natural close to a life when the person is dying. That's quite different to doctors prescribing a lethal dose to deliberately foreshorten life, sometimes by months but possibly by years – you just wouldn't know how much life had been cut off.

DISCUSSION

A game changer?

Charles Clarke   I think where I will begin is with Rob George. You used the word 'game-changer'. And Charlie, in your introduction you were talking about bringing the law in line with where the population is. Can I just ask all of you to what extent this is a game-changer? Is it going to change behaviour?

Charles Falconer   I think Rob is completely wrong because the way that I think the issue is perceived at the moment is that people go to Switzerland to die and there won't be any prosecution in relation to it. Ilora said, surprisingly, in her remarks that she was happy with that position. She also said, again I think completely wrongly, that in relation to all laws they're only enforced if the prosecuting authorities think it's a genuine hard case – that's nonsense. There is only one law where it is habitually not enforced and that is the law on assisting suicide.

Giles Fraser No, it's not a game-changer. What I'm interested in is the way in which people care for each other, and I think we're already so far down the route of people thinking that they're just individual autonomous objects that have rights over their own bodies, and they have the right to choose and it's just about them, and I think the 82% of people who say the individual has the right to choose how to die, that's where the bulk of the people are with this, and I think that's how they behave and what they're like. So I'm completely out of sympathy with that. I have a view in which the individual doesn't have such an important and prominent place, which is not a view that's popular at the moment. I don't think you have a right over your own body.

Ilora Finlay It's a complete game-changer, if you look at what's happened in those countries that have changed the law, and it's a small number of countries that have done. Holland was the first country to change its law. The number of deaths by euthanasia which is where the doctor is injecting or prescribing and supplying physician-assisted suicide has gone up so that it's now 1 in 37 of all deaths in the country. That would translate to something around about 13,000 a year in the UK.

The development of specialist palliative care in other countries just hasn't happened. You don't have the training programmes that you have here; you don't have the focus on driving up better end-of-life care. I've had many, many patients who have been signed-up members of the Voluntary Euthanasia Society, as it was, currently Dignity in Dying. They're frightened of dying. And I've had several who have said to me, 'I never believed I could have such good quality of life and have not gone on to pursue a request.'

Rob George I think there's no doubt that it is a game-changer. You've just got to look at the facts. The deaths per year in this country are in the order of half a million. The number of patients that I look after who talk about assisted suicide or talk about euthanasia is probably about 10%. I can count the number of people on two hands really over the years who've had specialist palliative care who then consistently want to end their lives. In my view the game changes because the attitudes and perspectives will start to affect clinicians.

Charles Falconer   I'm absolutely appalled by what Giles says, because Giles is saying that a group of people who might be suffering terribly, they've got to suffer as an example to everybody else so that people care for each other better in the future, which I think is an extraordinary proposition for the churches.

Giles Fraser   Their suffering is a part of life. I mean, that's the whole thing that's so nonsense about your position, the idea that you can somehow eliminate suffering from life.

Charles Falconer   And therefore you've got to go through it even if there are ways to bring it to an end?

Giles Fraser   It is what it is to be human, and care for the human is a part of that.

Charles Falconer   Then you're a brute.

Deciding what's right

Charles Clarke   I'm going to move now to this question of the person concerned knowing that they want to die and the issues around how we know they know. To what extent are doctors able to make the judgements that we're talking about in this area? Is it possible to get to a yes/no answer as to whether somebody really does want to be assisted to die, and will that really be what they want when the moment actually comes?

Giles Fraser   Now, I've got a PhD in Philosophy so I apologise I could go down that route for a very long time, but it is a problem. It is a problem how you know what you think you know you know. The truth of the matter is you can't know with something like this that you know what you know.

Ilora Finlay   I go from the experience of talking to a lot of patients. People fluctuate, people will talk about wanting to be dead, they don't want to go on, they wish they could end it all. And some may even attempt suicide themselves and will then later on go on to say how glad that they are still alive, how much meaning their life has. There is this fluctuation that you see in most people who become ill, that goes between hope and despair, and it's part of the adapting process to illness and to the potential loss of life that people are facing.

If I can just give you one story. A patient was referred to me with his GP saying, 'This is the most clear-cut case for euthanasia that I have ever come across.' He, a consultant surgeon, and a consultant oncologist all thought this chap would be dead within three months, and the patient was absolutely adamant that he wanted assistance to end his life. I thought he would be dead in three months as well.

Many years later he said, 'Just don't go there. What would have happened to my kids?' Because his wife then died and he ended up as a sole parent, by then in a wheelchair, still with his horrible disease ongoing. He's brought these children up himself. He will talk to me very openly about the despair he felt when he thought that he was dying, he didn't want to be a burden. But his life has huge meaning, and we have to come out the other side.

Rob George   You've just seen in the interaction between Charlie and Ilora the difference between a lawyer and a clinician. The lawyers are all about switches on and off, yeses and nos; we're all about maybe, don't really know, let's see how it goes. Because life is like that, the complexities and the sophistications.

I just want to address the coercion question. There is necessarily coercion involved. Are you seriously going to be wanting to get a doctor to come and assess and evaluate you for assisted suicide who likes doing it? No, you're going to want a doctor who does it reluctantly. The word reluctantly means they're coerced into doing it. And one of our duties, and we can be hung up by the toe nails for violating this, is not to do harm to people.

And one thing I know beyond anything else having practised as long as I have is that I don't know the future, I really don't. I do not know how somebody's going to change, but I do know that when bad things happen to people they usually change, and as often as not they change for the good. I'm not suggesting therefore that suffering is inherently a good thing, I'm saying that suffering is part of the human condition. It's the way it is, and generally the older you get the wiser you become because of all the bad things that have happened along the way. If we amputate that experience from people we turn them into robots.

Charles Falconer Ilora, Giles and Rob are saying assisted dying is too difficult to do. There are two bits to it.

First of all, do you believe that people are able to come to the conclusion in a context of a terminal illness that having thought about it, having discussed it, they do want to die? The evidence we got in the Commission for Assisted Dying is that there were a small group of people, no matter how much you gave them excellent palliative care, no matter how much you tried to dissuade them, who would be determined not to go on with the sort of consequences of the particular terminal illness they had. There are people in the world who are capable and keen to reach a conclusion about whether or not they want their life to end in the context of a terminal illness.

And then there are Rob and Ilora's doctors never knowing what's going to happen. They're saying nothing is certain, and they're obviously right, but as they will both acknowledge in relation to the way that palliative care is delivered, in the way that medicine is delivered, you do have to make decisions from time to time and generally they will be right. Yes, there may be occasions where they're wrong, but when you're treating a patient you have to reach some conclusions. And I think it will be a very mighty decision in an individual case, people will be careful about doing it.

But we should not step back from this on the basis that it's just too difficult, nobody can make up their own mind, and doctors don't know what's going on. I think that's a completely wrong-headed way of looking at it.

Leaders of opinion

Charles Clarke Linda demonstrated that the majority of Members of Parliament are not in favour of the change. The view of Rob and Ilora is that most doctors would not be in favour of the change. Giles has the view that most church leaders would not be in favour of a change. But at the same time, despite these leaders of opinion not favouring change, the vast majority of people faced with the question do favour change. Why do you think there is this difference, and does that difference have any significance?

Rob George I think that doctors have gone into the job to help people to live until they die and look after people while they die and not to do it in order that they die. I think that there's a fundamental underlying revulsion among clinicians actively to bring about death, and I don't see clinicians weeping into their beer in the pub after work because their patients aren't dead.

Charles Falconer My experience from doing the Commission on Assisted Dying was that most doctors were in the position where they said we don't mind whether you say yes or whether you say no to it, but please make your mind up because you're so confused. They did not have a strong view one way or the other. They wanted certainty as to what the position was, but there were also two groups, one who was very much in favour of it and one who's very much against it.

In relation to the church, the Anglican Church and the Roman Catholic Church are very much against it, but interestingly enough not on moral grounds. They're against it on practical grounds, which I find quite mysterious. As far as Members of Parliament are concerned, I've never been an MP but I would imagine that whether or not you're going to be elected as an MP or not is not going to be dependent on whether or not a few people support you because you support assisted dying, but because organised religion is against it it's a quite dangerous position to take up. And secondly the Commons has avoided for the last five years ever having a debate about it because by and large MPs don't want to take up a position because of the politics of it.

Ilora Finlay Politicians look at legislation. Those responsible for passing legislation look to see whether it is safe to pass the law and can see when they look at the so-called safeguards that it's too dangerous – you can't define things clearly enough in black and white to make it safe.

In terms of the population out there, fear is certainly a major opinion former, and those who go to church and are adherents to religion read the newspapers and watch the media just like those who don't, and get the same information as they do, and are understandably frightened by the stories that they read. The difficulty is that the reality that we are working to provide is not newsworthy. If you look at palliative care patients' experience, we've got four years' data from across the whole of Wales, all specialist palliative care services all scoring above 9.5 out of 10 on nine main domains repeatedly. No press interest in that whatsoever.

Giles Fraser The one thing I imagine the three of us share is that we've seen a lot of dying and dead people, a lot of them. And I think we live in a society that's absolutely petrified of death and dying in a way we never really used to be. We live in all sorts of fictions and we want to get it out of sight and out of mind, and I think what the lawyer wants to do here is put it out of sight and out of mind because he doesn't realise that the reality of death can be faced and it's okay.

Body, mind and spirit

Sue Radford I was brought up to believe that the human being was made up of body, mind and spirit. I think a lot of the debate deals with the body and the mind, which are decaying for whatever reason. But in terms of the spirit, how do you allow the spirit journey to continue because the spiritual journey, the soul journey, isn't over until it's over, and I'm sure many people on the panel, especially Giles and those in palliative care, will have been around people who in their final days have had some quite remarkable experiences on this spiritual journey. I saw it with my father who had dementia, my mother-in-law who died of terminal cancer – they had remarkable journeys, which was also a great comfort to those who are left behind.

Jonathan Romaine I'd also like to pick up on the religious aspect. I speak as a rabbi in favour of assisted dying and part of a new alliance of clergy across all faiths who think we can believe in the sanctity of life, but we don't believe in the sanctity of suffering. Of course, as Giles said, suffering is part of life, but there's also a duty to lessen it as much as possible. Isn't it actually rather arrogant to deny that option to those people who are terminally ill and suffering and who wish it. The idea of keeping someone else alive so that you can keep your principles intact, isn't that very self-centred?

Rob George In respect of the spiritual side of things, what I have found in looking after patients is that patients who believe, think, feel and say the same thing will by and large have a peaceful death. It's internal conflict that leads to existential crisis.

On the arrogance question, if we think it is arrogant, then what on earth are we doing legislating for doctors who don't want to do it? Actually, what we should do is have a shelf in Sainsbury's saying, 'Taking the following medicine will seriously damage your health', or making gas available or something like that … If we genuinely believed that this was a good thing for society, we should just legislate and say this is available, that's where you go and get the stuff. To put it behind the laundry of healthcare and somehow make it okay is disingenuous. Where the arrogance lies is that society is not willing to take responsibility for itself.

Ilora Finlay Sue's comments made me think of Cicely Saunders' statement, which is that the way a person dies lives on in the memory of those left behind. And certainly the spiritual, existential domain of people is an important part of who they are and the way that they respond to their physical and other emotional pressures too. To Rabbi Jonathan I would simply say that I'm really worried if you think that doctors have to keep someone alive at all costs because that's not the case at all. We don't. People can refuse treatment, but we have a duty of care, we do have to redouble our efforts to relieve suffering.

Charles Falconer I think the spiritual journey, from my much more limited experience of being with people when they are dying, is incredibly important. But the spiritual journey doesn't necessarily coincide with the physical journey. As far as Jonathan Romaine's remarks are concerned, I must say I had exactly the same reaction as you did Jonathan to that sort of wagging a finger and laying down the law and saying you've got to suffer so that society's better as a community. I thought we'd moved on from that.

Giles Fraser I'm not a fundamentalist on the issue of suffering, and there are times when I would imagine taking the draught myself. But what I worry about in a broader sense is that it's not about me liking suffering, it's about wanting to suck up as much reality as possible into life, and I think that if you avoid suffering you hold down other things. With regard to the question of the spiritual journey and that bit at the end of life, it's very interesting that in the Middle Ages if you'd asked people how they wanted to die it wouldn't be quietly, quickly and in your sleep, it would actually be to take a bit of time. Because they needed to say goodbye to their families, they needed to say goodbye to their enemies, they needed to make peace with the world and themselves, and they needed to prepare themselves for death. It's not that I value suffering, it's that I value human beings, and human beings suffer.

SOME MEDIA REACTION

Most religious followers support assisted suicide for the dying.
British Medical Journal, 2 May 2013

A new poll finds overwhelming support for assisted suicide for the terminally ill among Anglicans, Catholics, Hindus, Sikhs and Jews in Britain, with Baptists and Muslims the only groups that oppose changes to British law, which currently prohibits assisted suicide.
Washington Post, 2 May 2013

'We are used to having more control over our lives and I think that is partly why there is this overwhelming number of people saying that they have a right to decide for themselves.'
Linda Woodhead, quoted by BBC News, 1 May 2013

A major survey of religious opinion shows that large majorities of believers are in favour of legalising assisted dying … Christian groups reacted with dismay to the results …

Austen Ivereigh, of the lobby group Catholic Voices, said: 'It shows how little exposed even practising religious people are to the teachings of their church. I can only remember hearing three homilies on the subject in all my years in church.' A Church of England spokesman said: 'This study demonstrates that complex discussions on topics such as assisted suicide and euthanasia cannot be effectively conducted through the medium of online surveys.'

Andrew Brown, *Guardian*, 30 April 2013

Summary: **WHAT HAVE WE LEARNED?** by **LINDA WOODHEAD**

- Of all our debates in this series on religion and personal life, this is the one which is the most 'live' and unresolved. Same-sex marriage is also hotly contested at the moment, and for some time there has been a gap between the law and public opinion on the issue, but the gap was only small, and it looks as if it will be closed very soon. But in relation to euthanasia the gap between the law and opinion is very large, and it is not at all clear that it will be closed in the near future.
- In this debate most of the speakers were opposed to any change in the law on euthanasia. Both of the palliative care specialists, Ilora Finlay and Rob George, produced a raft of arguments against assisted dying:

  - it is impossible to predict when someone will die
  - people cannot be certain that they really wish to die
  - most suffering can be controlled and we are unnecessarily frightened of dying
  - most people who go through the natural process of dying benefit from so doing, often to their surprise
  - it is wrong to make physicians responsible for helping people to die, and this changes the whole nature of the medical profession
  - if euthanasia is allowed, some people will feel pressured to die.

● Giles Fraser offered another argument against euthanasia – that our society overplays the importance of freedom of choice, and underplays the importance of suffering. We should not seek autonomy and control, but should embrace a human condition which includes finitude, failure, loss of dignity and connection with others.

● Charles Falconer was the only speaker to argue for a change in the law – to permit physician-assisted dying under certain tightly controlled conditions. He argued that this change is needed in order to bring the law into line with what people are actually doing (having to travel to Switzerland to die) and to make the situation more humane. He argued that if we can help people avoid terrible suffering in the final stages of life, we ought to do so.

● This debate, and the survey findings, attracted a great deal of public and media interest. Most discussed was the finding that so many religious people support a change in the law. This surprised people who had assumed that because most religions officially oppose euthanasia so strongly most religious people would follow suit. That is clearly not the case. Recently the churches have devoted much more energy to opposing same-sex marriage than euthanasia. Perhaps that will change. In any case, of all the issues we have looked at in the book, this is likely to be the one around which the most active debate will occur in the future.

DISCUSSION QUESTIONS

1. If the law were changed to allow assisted dying, could we trust friends, family and doctors always to respect our wishes and act in our best interests?

2. Do you think that the sacredness of human life is a good reason for keeping the law unchanged and not allowing euthanasia?

3. Should the wishes of those who do not want the option of assisted dying stand in the way of those who do?

4. Would it change your view on legislating for assisted dying if no members of the medical profession were obliged or allowed to play a part?

5. Can anyone really know that they want to die?
6. What do you think the limits are – if any – on my right to do what I want with my own life?

RESOURCES

View the debate at www.faith debates.org.uk.

Read the BBC online Ethics Guide to Religion and Euthanasia at bbc. co.uk/ethics/euthanesia/religion.sntml.

Dignity in Dying is a UK-based organisation campaigning for choice, access and control to alleviate suffering at the end of life, offering information and personal stories.

The final report of the Commission on Assisted Dying is available at http://www.commissiononassisteddying.co.uk/.

'Considering the evidence', report from Living and Dying Well, http:// www.livinganddyingwell.org.uk/publications/our-reports/considering-the-evidence, is critical of physician-assisted euthanasia.

Assisted Dying for the Terminally Ill Bill – Select Committee Report (Vol. 1), HMSO, 2005; http://www.parliament.uk/business/committees/committees-a-z/former-committees/lords-select/assisted-dying-for-the-terminally-ill-bill/publications/.

Ilora Finlay and Rob George, 'Legal physician-assisted suicide in Oregon and The Netherlands: Evidence concerning the impact on patients in vulnerable groups – another perspective on Oregon's data', *Journal of Medical Ethics* 37 (2011), pp. 171–74.

Ilora Finlay, 'Laws have to be designed to work safely in the real world', *The Times*, 16 May 2013.

CHAPTER SEVEN

Why do God?
Delia Smith and Alastair Campbell in conversation

I believe in a personal God. I don't think this can be communicated by another person ... I do know that deep down in everybody there is this capacity for God.
Delia Smith

I'm a pro-faith atheist ... I can't make that intellectual leap that says all of these things that I think, and the life that I think people should lead, and the values that they should hold, that I'm going to wrap them in something called God or anything else you might want to call it.
Alastair Campbell

Opening comment by **CHARLES CLARKE**

This final chapter differs a little from the previous ones because it took the form of an interview and conversation between two people rather than a larger debate.

We devised the idea of the Westminster Faith Interviews to try and illuminate the nature of religious belief through discussions about it. I found that the interview between Delia Smith and Alastair Campbell, both friends of mine, did that very well, and it's also a really good read.

For me, two exchanges are particularly interesting. The first deals with the power of God, the question which concerns so many atheists: If God is so powerful, powerful enough to create the world, how does he allow so many terrible things to happen?

Alastair But if he's so powerful why can't he do it? …

Delia OK, let's try another way. You're a father and you've got a beloved child and that child has to have a mind of its own and a will of its own and, as a loving father, which I know you are, you want that child to have everything to succeed. But you can't go and do it for them, they've got to do it for themselves.

Delia's metaphorical answer has, for me, the great virtue that she emphasises the responsibility which people have for their own destiny, their need to work to create a world in which we can be proud. It addresses the debilitating fatalism which suggests some kind of Calvinist predestination which determines our lives.

And the other exchange relates to the often difficult relationship between politics and religion. Alastair Campbell famously used the phrase 'We don't do God' and during this debate explained how that came about:

Alastair The 'We don't do God' thing came about, because … after 9/11 we were travelling all over the world. A writer from *Vanity Fair* was writing a massive profile about Tony. He kept saying to me, 'I just want some minutes with Tony Blair' … and eventually I said, 'Right, come down the plane, you've got 20 minutes, you can sit and have a cup of tea with him and talk about anything you want.' And he was like a lot of journalists … 'One more question. Prime Minister, that's a really interesting answer; just one more question if I may.' We were on the eleventh 'one more question' when he said, 'Finally, finally, finally, if I may Prime Minister, my very, very, very final question, I'd like to ask you about your faith.'

And I stepped in, and I said, 'I'm sorry, we don't do God.' That was it.

He wrote his profile and it was there. The *Daily Telegraph* picked it up and they did a little piece, 'Alastair Campbell on why Blair doesn't do God,' and it just went whoosh.

That little story demonstrates the way in which small exchanges can influence the way in which political and religious discussion can be perceived in the modern media era. It makes the case for genuine discussion about these matters and the need to take religion very seriously for what it is, not what it is not.

DELIA SMITH[1] AND ALASTAIR CAMPBELL[2]

 Knowing God

Alastair I do know you through football and journalism really, which are not the two most Godly parts of our national life. But I was amazed, genuinely, when I went off and found these books [Delia's books on spirituality, see note 1] and read them and learnt how fundamental your faith would seem to be. I want to start by asking you to define your relationship with God.

Delia I believe that God is the creator of everything. I'm bowled over by that for a start. Secondly, the thing that I suppose moves me the most now is the phenomenon of human life. I cannot believe it's all an accident, and 'life's a bitch and then you die', as somebody said. And I think that human life is elevated to being co-creator with God.

---

[1] Delia Smith CBE is a best-selling cookery writer, and has been a TV cookery celebrity for almost four decades. She is also known for her spiritual books. A Roman Catholic convert at age 22, she has published *A Feast for Lent* (2nd edn, BRF, 1991), *A Feast for Advent* (BRF, 2006), and *A Journey into God* (2nd edn, Hodder & Stoughton, 1993), a book on prayer. Another of her great passions is football, becoming in 1996 a Director of Norwich City ('The Canaries'). With her husband Michael Wynn Jones, they are now Joint Majority Shareholders in this Premier League club.

[2] Alastair Campbell is best known for his role as spokesman, press secretary and director of communications and strategy for Prime Minister Tony Blair (1997–2003). He is well known for interrupting an interview with Tony Blair with the words, 'We don't do God'. He is currently a writer, communicator and strategist, and champions the cause of The Leukaemia and Lymphoma Research Fund.

Alastair   Now, let's say that your parents hadn't been your parents but they'd been a Saudi prince and a Saudi princess and you'd been born there and raised in that culture. You'd have a totally different sort of life, but you might be sitting there saying that you believe in God, but it's a totally different God and it's a totally different vision of God. Are you more right than they are?

Delia   No, but I believe in a personal God. I don't think this can be communicated by another person. I really do believe that within every person there is, whether they admit it or not, there is what the church calls 'the seed of eternity', but I'd like to call it a little smouldering fire. I do know that deep down in everybody there is this capacity for God.

Alastair   Why have you got it and I haven't?

Delia   Do you want me to tell you how I got my faith? By accident, totally and utterly by accident. When I was young, about five years old, my parents didn't have any religion. But my mother used to put me to bed too early. And she gave me an old-fashioned Victorian picture of Jesus with children all around him, all different colours and nationalities, and she said to me, 'Jesus looks after children and you pray to him.' And she taught me how to say the Our Father.

So there am I in bed, broad daylight, not being able to sleep, and there was this picture, and I thought about it more and more. And it just happened that every night when I went to bed there was this time of stillness and silence and reflection. Now, reflection is a very, very important word and I think that reflection is something that we don't think enough about. If you have space and time to develop your reflective powers, which we all have, then you get in touch with something deep. If we're talking about God we have to talk about deep. We have surface life and we have deep life.

So once reflection develops, we can understand and go deep,

so there's this part of our lives, the deep part, the real me, the person. It's there that I, if you like, begin to understand God.

Alastair   But I feel I go deep and I reflect but I don't have your faith. Why is my deepness any less significant than yours?

Delia   Well, maybe because you don't want it and are not pursuing it. In the scriptures it says the wise men came from the east and they searched diligently; well, that's me. I have searched diligently.

Alastair   I'm interested in God.

Delia   Great!

Alastair   Right, but I'm interested in God from an intellectual point of view. You probably can't quite see why I can't see it and I can't really see why you see it.

I love the bit in the book where you say that God talks through his sources close to. What does that mean?

Delia   Well I think what happens in a deeply reflective life is that a little light goes on. I've never had a religious experience, never, but a little light goes on and things resonate. I'm taken up now with thinking about the whole evolutionary process and how exciting it all is that the human race is moving forward and progressing.

Alastair   Is God guiding that?

Delia   Yes and no. I think we are co-creators, we are co-creators with God. So if I can be really simplistic, God says, 'Right there, human family, off you go. I'm here with you to help you, but you go and conquer that universe, you go and do it.'

Alastair   But if he's so powerful, why can't he do it? A co-creator sounds a bit blasphemous to me.

Delia   Okay, let's try another way. You're a father and you've got a beloved child and that child has to have a mind of its own and a will of its own, and as a loving father, which I know you are, you want that child to have everything to succeed. But you can't go and do it for them, they've got to do it for themselves.

Alastair   Okay, I get that.
      You talk about prayer. This is the other thing I thought was really interesting. I know the books were written a long time ago, so you may have changed, but my sense is you see prayer not as an act but as a process, a never-ending process, almost like a state of mind. Is that right?

Delia   Where I've moved on now is that I don't like the word prayer. I think people get very confused and think they can't pray. I just think if you want to know God, if you want to have a sense of God, then I think you need to have reflective time in your life, and I think you then have to just be open to it, and watch this little light going on. And it's not in, you know, religious things, it's in life, it's every day.

Alastair   So are you praying now?

Delia   Every day in my life I have stillness and silence, every day.

Alastair   And how do you do that?

Delia   I have half an hour in the morning and half an hour in the evening.

Alastair   And where do you go and what do you do?

Delia   Well, I'm very lucky because I have something called a writer's tree house at the bottom of the garden and I can go there, but, I mean, it's possible anywhere. Now, I don't know how to pray, I haven't got a clue.

Alastair So what do you do?

Delia The onus is not on me, but what I do is I just sit down. My mind is full of all kinds of distractions, whatever it is, but it doesn't matter. I just find this silent time – it's receptivity.

Alastair But are you spending time with yourself or with God?

Delia Well, I believe that God is present in every human person.

Alastair And are you talking?

Delia No, there's no talking and no conversation.

Alastair Do you see somebody or something?

Delia No nothing, nothing.

Alastair Do you hear anything?

Delia No, it's really boring, it's very boring.

Alastair So it could be like meditation.

Delia No, none of those grand ... They're too grandiose, no, I'm not clever enough.

Challenges to faith

Alastair What about bad things? Where does that fit in?

Take a fairly topical aspect of modern human life, which is people citing faith to justify acts of killing and of terror. Now, what does your God make of all that? The guy who's flying the plane into the twin towers, one of his last thoughts was that he was doing it for God, and when he dies he's going to go off to heaven and the virgins are all going to wait for him, and that's making him feel really good about it. I can't get my head round that.

Delia   No, I can't either, but I do think this whole evolutionary process is that we are evolving, and on the way we are striving, we are making mistakes, people are getting the wrong end of the stick.

Alastair   Where does it end?

Delia   It ends in human beings, individual human beings, becoming one and being united with God. I think we're evolving towards love and at the moment we're not perhaps very near it but that's …

Alastair   Is that a way of just keeping the world going for ever, in that we're never ever going to get to that position?

Delia   No, because I think we will. Here we have to go now to the trickiest bit of all.

Alastair   Go on.

Delia   The creator God who created the universe, all of life and human life, is involved in that human life like a father is involved in a son. We're told to say Father, our Father. Human life is so important and so precious that this God of ours took on becoming human to experience what we experience, and to join us in our journey.

Alastair   So all that is just part of a journey?

Delia   Yes.

Alastair   So when you do come out of your half-hour at the bottom of the garden and you turn on the telly or the radio and it is all bad news –

Delia   It's horrible. I don't want to see it. I'm a coward.

Alastair   Right, but it is part of a journey.

Delia   I'm a coward and I don't want to see it, but it's part of the pain of entering our destiny, part of the pain of it is suffering.

Alastair   Okay, I'll buy that.

Delia   Okay, because the way they say it in the Bible is quite a good way. The labourer in the vineyard is suffering in the hot sun, labouring away, and then at the end of it there's this beautiful wine in the bottle and I think we're nowhere near it, but we're getting there, and hope is a very important thing.

Alastair   You said in your book *Journey into God* that the sole purpose of our existence is union with God.

Delia   Yes, union with each other and union with God.

Alastair   Well, can you have one without the other? I can sign up to the first bit. But what does that mean if I can't do that, if I can't have that union with God?

Delia   But you can.

Alastair   But if I decide I can't, for whatever reason.

Delia   Well, that's your choice. If you choose not to choose, then that's your choice.

Alastair   Right, but does that mean that I'm worthless because there's then no point in my existence?

Delia   No, because unity, complete unity between all that exists, is complete unity. So though I believe everyone is completely individual, I believe that we're all one, so that we'll go to our destiny as one and we'll say, 'Come on Alastair, you're one with us now', so I'm afraid you're here.

Alastair   But you're sort of dragging me along, I haven't made that leap in my heart.

Delia   No, no, we're not dragging you along because it'll be all right. It'll be all right on the night!

Alastair   I'm not one of those militant atheists, I don't like all that.

Delia   No I know, no I know you're not, and you're very understanding. But perhaps I'd better tell you one of the most significant things that happened to me. In the 60s when I became a Catholic, there were books on sale by a priest scientist called Teilhard de Chardin. He was a palaeontologist, a geologist and a very accomplished scientist, and he started something which I think now is the future, and that is the convergence of science and religion.

Alastair   But there have always been scientists who have got a deep faith.

Delia   He was a priest in the First World War, and he chose to be a stretcher-bearer. Everything came from that experience. I just hope one publisher somewhere in the world will publish all these books again here now. You know, the whole computer thing, the web, I think it's happening, it's going to happen to us, it's happening to us. We are converging and there are signs of it.

Alastair   Where do you stand on issues like women bishops?

Delia [laughs] I knew this one was coming. Oh! Well, unfortunately churches, they drag their feet a bit don't they? Obviously you've got to have women priests and if you've got women priests then you've got to have women bishops. And the Catholic Church has never yet come up with anything I've read that says why you can't. They say you can't, but they haven't said why you can't. Now, as an observer of religious things and religious people and I go to Mass every day and I think …

Alastair You go every day?

Delia Yes. And I think that I probably wouldn't have any priests at all. See what I would have, I mean this is me now – I know I'm going to get a letter from the bishop in the morning saying, 'Don't appear in public any more, you're banned'! – but I think that observing this over all these years, priests are one-man bands you know, or they're married, but either way there's a problem. So what I would do is have a shared ministry. I would have somebody who maybe is ordained to say mass and administer the sacraments, but alongside him, if you're good at preaching, you would be a preacher …

Alastair Or her.

Delia … or her, yes. If you were good at counselling, you'd be a counsellor. If you had time to visit the sick you would visit the sick. If you're an accountant you'd do the accounts and if you're good at, I don't know, if you're a handyman you can look after the building.

Alastair [to audience] She's talking wholesale modernisation of the church.

Delia I am, yes.

Alastair And how far are we down that evolutionary path?

Delia   I'm too old. If I could have been Pope it would have all been different.

Alastair   [laughing] Would you have liked to have been the Pope?

Delia   I'd like to have been the Pope, and I'd like to be the Head of the Football Association!

Alastair   She's just power crazy like the rest of us.

Football

Charles Clarke   The one thing I wanted to ask Delia is, through football and the rest of it, you've constantly talked about how society should give more importance to those sort of things, to allow the individual to come through. Could you just talk a little bit about that?

Delia   Well, given that I believe the whole world is moving towards being more social, I think that my experience of football is it gives you an experience of community like nothing else. I think human beings are at their very best when they're in community.

Alastair   But didn't the church used to do that?

Delia   Yes, and it still does. I can find mass all over the world. That's community, so I can find my community in Germany, Holland, France or Dubai. But I think football is perhaps equal to that, because in fact if I travel round the world all I've got to do is find somebody who likes football and I'm off, and I've got companionship. That's how we're made, we're made to have a collective passion and we're meant to be together and support one another.

CONVERSATION WITH THE AUDIENCE

 Choosing faith

Chris Rich I'm a priest who's out of a job now. Delia, do you think there's a difference between choosing faith and accepting faith?

Delia Choosing it – you see, I got it by accident so I don't actually have an experience of choosing it. But I think accepting it is probably very important. Somebody once wrote about empty spaces that only God can fill, and I think acceptance and receptivity are very important. Does that answer it or not?

Chris Rich It does, but you were saying to Alastair that his not having faith is a choice.

Delia I think it probably is. I think if I hadn't come to it in the way I came to it I'd want to be able to find out about it and really know about it before I could reject it.

Alastair I think that it's not that I've rejected it. I'm a pro-faith atheist; I mean, I brought along my book for Delia today because there's a bit in there I'd forgotten until someone reminded me this morning, where I talk about this, what I think is a near religious experience after a friend of mine died, and all this nature stuff going on, and – well, it's too complicated to explain now.

But the point is that I can feel all that and I do feel all that, but I don't, I can't, make that intellectual leap that says all of these things that I think, and the life that I think people should lead, and the values that they should hold, that I'm going to wrap them in something called God or anything else you might want to call it.

[The story of Jesus] is probably the most told and retold story on the planet in the history of the world and it's a very, very powerful story.

I think you have to have priests by the way. I'm re-hiring this guy. I think you have to have priests and I think you have to have words and you have to know what you think those words mean. I don't think you can have a redefinition of God, Jesus …

Linda Woodhead People don't just use 'God' now, but those words do change, so as many people believe in 'Spirit' or 'energy', as use the word God. It's not always fixed.

Alastair Well, maybe they do, but I think they are moving away from a set of beliefs then, or they're adapting a set of beliefs.

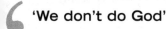

'We don't do God'

Linda Woodhead Alastair, I've got to ask you about 'doing God'. If you think about the Labour Government in your time, in some ways it was incredibly religious, it had a deep kind of Christian socialist belief. You remember *Private Eye* depicted Tony Blair as 'Vicar of St Albion'. There was that sense about Tony Blair, and yet it's only out of office that he 'came out' about his faith. Gordon Brown also came out. So at the time there was a keeping the lid on doing God. Why, and was it necessary?

Alastair Well, I'll tell you why. As to whether it was necessary your judgement is as valid as mine on that. I'll tell you the history of the thing. I always knew that Tony Blair was somebody of faith. I didn't know until I got to know Tony really well just how big a part of his life it was. We had to find a church everywhere we went and it was a bloody nightmare because of security and all the rest of it, but we did, and that's part of what we had to do – as if we didn't have enough to get on with!

I always said to him that whereas in America you can't really become President unless you were seen every Sunday wandering around clutching the Bible, I always felt rightly or wrongly that a politician in our system who emphasised his or her religious faith was taking a political risk because they were laying themselves open for the accusation that they were aligning their politics with their faith.

The only time that Tony actually – how dare he! – went against me and wrote on this issue, he wrote a piece for the *Sunday Telegraph* (I can't remember when, 1995 or 1996). It was about 'What Easter means to me' by Tony Blair. It was a very interesting, very thoughtful, very personal, very compelling piece. And I said to him, 'Well, do it if you really want to do it, but I'm telling you the news on Sunday's going to lead with the Tories saying that you are claiming that to believe in God you have to be Labour.' And he said, 'But I'm not saying that at all.' I said, 'I know you're not saying that, but I promise you that is what is going to happen.'

Delia   That's what they'll do.

Alastair   And do you know who the two were who led the charge? Brian Mahwinney and Anne Widdecombe! They're both big believers! The politics of it were messy. Tony accepted that thereafter.

Charles Clarke   He accepted you were right?

Alastair   He accepted I was right, yes, you're absolutely right, Charles.

The other thing I must tell you is how that 'We don't do God' thing came about, because it's the most ridiculous story. I promise you that, including today, there is not a day I don't get emails and letters from people saying, 'I'm writing a thesis about this, you said "We don't do God", what was the strategic thinking behind this?'

I'll tell you exactly what happened. It was after 9/11. We were travelling all over the world. There was a guy from *Vanity Fair* called David Margolick, very well-known profile writer, he was writing a massive profile about Tony. And he was coming all over the world with us, he was on the plane, he was hanging around, and he kept saying to me, 'I just want just some minutes with Tony Blair.' I kept promising him. 'Yes, we'll do it, yes we'll do it,' fobbing him off, fobbing him off. We were on a flight to America. Eventually I said, 'Right, come down the plane, you've got 20 minutes, you can sit and have a cup of tea with him and talk about anything you want.'

And he was like a lot of journalists – I've done it, we've all done it: 'One more question. Prime Minister, that's a really interesting answer, just one more question if I may.' We were on the eleventh 'one more question' when he said, 'Finally, finally, finally, if I may Prime Minister, my very, very, very final question, I'd like to ask you about your faith.'

And I stepped in, and I said, 'I'm sorry, we don't do God.' That was it. That was it.

He wrote his profile and it was there. The *Daily Telegraph* picked it up and they did a little piece low down on page 7 or something, 'Alastair Campbell on why Blair doesn't do God,' and it just went whoosh.

I still think for a British politician there's a danger. So it's not that I didn't believe in what the government did, but I think it's possible to believe in what the government you're working for is doing without thinking that it's all about 'God and my right'.

Speaking of faith

Charles Clarke Delia, how easy do you find it to talk about your faith? One of the things we've found in these Westminster Faith Debates is that many people somehow don't find it easy to talk about their faith. You had to decide this evening whether you'd be ready to come and talk about it, and you've done so extremely openly. Have you done that throughout your life?

Delia Yes. The problem is somebody shutting me up!

Alastair   But do you think that people of faith feel slightly beleaguered? I get that impression. Because of all the Dawkins stuff and John Humphrys and the kind of 'anti-Godism' that's around the place.

Delia   Yes I do, and that's why I'm going to have a try at writing something else.

Mark Chater   Can I just ask you about doing God in schools, just tell us a bit about your views on to what extent in this society we can and should speak about God in schools and ask questions about God in schools?

Delia   Well, as a 5-year-old convert, I really feel there should be instruction, and I think children should be brought up to know what it's all about. I'm in favour of a multi-cultural society and the global village, and we have to learn about other faiths as well. But I do think it's very sad if there is no education at all and children today are surprised when they hear about what Christians believe.

Alastair   I favour the teaching of religion in schools, and by that I mean all religions and all faiths. In a sense the political class in Britain pays lip service to this. You know, Charles didn't ever stand up and say 'I'm not saying these silly prayers because I don't believe in God' … you go along with it.

When kids go to school we teach them that sport is a good thing for them. I think we should teach them that politics is a good thing, and I think we should teach them that having an interest in faith is a good thing as well.

I don't like faith schools, I don't like the idea that there's only one religion that can get taught in a school. I think we should teach children about faith and religion because I think it's a really important part of the modern world, not least because it's an important part of global politics at the moment.

Has society lost its moral compass?

Michael Barry At a previous Westminster Faith Debate, Baroness Williams spoke about a loss of moral compass at every level of British society. I was wondering, do you both agree and, if so, what do you mean by it?

Delia In a way, I just believe in the goodness of people and I don't know how you define it really. How do you define what morality is? I just believe that goodness will always win through. We get a lot of media and information about things that are not moral, but we get not enough about all the wonderful things that go on, and all the beauty and the creative combining of people, and I just feel I have faith that we will always move forward, we will always move on in the right direction.

Alastair I think the question does come partly from the culture of negativity that we live in, that we're surrounded by the whole time. In 1974 the positive–negative ratio in the British media was 3 to 1. In 2003 it was 1 to 18. Now, that is not just the national newspapers, it's not just the *Daily Mail*, it's across the board, it's a cultural shift. I'd love to know what these stories are when Delia turns on the radio and Ping! there was something wonderful happened – it's very rare that.

But I think you've got to be careful in distinguishing between a culture of negativity, for which we're all partly responsible because we all consume this stuff, and saying that therefore the people in positions of leadership display a loss of basic morality. I think there are still an awful lot of good people doing an awful lot of good things, I just don't think they get as big a voice as they used to.

Linda Woodhead Shirley Williams felt surprisingly strongly about this 'loss of moral compass', and she was talking about leadership in society, about banking, about politics, about the police – she feels something has gone wrong at the highest levels.

Alastair I think there's been bad in all of these organisations right down to the beginning of time, but I think we only really hear about the bad now. For example, take something like Parliament and MP's expenses. We all know about the moat and the mortgage fiddles and the rest of it. It was done by a minority of MPs, some of whom have gone to jail. Most MPs do a good job. I think the banks was an interesting one. I think football's interesting as well. I think Delia and I won't be too far apart. I actually feel there is a kind of immoral streak to the way that modern British football has developed.

Delia Money.

Alastair Yes, totally, all about money. And yet there are very good people, including at the top level of football. So compass and leadership – I don't know; I think most people have still got a pretty good moral compass.

Charles Clarke Delia, why don't you just talk for a couple of minutes on your approach to football? You talked to me about it a lot and it completely endorses what Alastair has said.

Delia Well, I just think it's very sad that money took over. And the creation of the Premier League really has been its downfall. Because certain canny chairmen saw that the Sky money was coming and thought, 'Well, let's make a special league and take all the money.' And the rest of football is scrabbling about trying to make ends meet. I've been there. And the money that's all washing about in this one league is going out to the rest of the world to bring in foreign players and our players in the lower leagues haven't got a chance. I mean, we, Norwich, last year when we played Liverpool, they'd just bought somebody, and the whole squad of Norwich was about half that guy's wages.

You've got this top six, and they're never going to change because it's all about money, so I do think that's wrong. And I think it has incredible implications for society. Football, I always call it the safe drug; young guys going to football letting off steam is better than them out on the streets doing knife crimes and taking drugs, and I think all governments have missed a trick here by not sorting football out and not threatening to regulate it if it doesn't sort itself out. The average age of the football attendee now is 47 or something, and you can see where it's going. It's going! It'll only be on television. So it is a problem.

Is the Bible literally true?

[Name not given] You spoke very favourably about scripture and how it's influenced you, but is there any scripture you reject? I mean for example the Adam and Eve story and the idea that human life started 6,000 years ago according to Genesis. Do you accept every word in the scripture?

Delia I don't reject it, but I don't read scripture as if every line is the truth. There are stories, there are myths, and I don't believe the world was created in seven days. I'm a total believer in evolution, but if I read the first chapter of Genesis it moves me because it's saying something, it's symbolising something very profound.

Whenever I get to that line that says male and female he made them, it always kind of catches something in me and I think how beautiful it is. I don't believe every word, and I think you have to look at it collectively, but I think there are very profound books in the Bible, and very profound things there. Particularly Paul's letters and John's Gospel in a good modern translation.

Alastair Is there faith in your cooking?

Delia I always used to say that I think God wants to help people with their cooking, and yes the celebration of life is the celebration of good food and good wine. It's all through the Bible and it's all through history, there is such enormous pleasure in eating.

MEDIA REACTION

Why do God? Because Alastair Campbell doesn't? Last night Tony Blair's former spin doctor was talking to celebrity cook Delia Smith about faith at Bloomsbury's BMA HQ and explained how his famous declaration has had unforeseen repercussions. 'It's the most ridiculous story,' said Campbell, 'and including today there has not been a day that I haven't had an email from someone saying "I'm writing a thesis about this and you said 'We don't do God'...".'

London Evening Standard, 6 December 2012

DISCUSSION QUESTIONS

1. Is faith in God (or lack of faith) a matter of choice, or is it something which grows out of experience over which you do not have control?
2. How serious a problem for belief is the existence of evil?
3. What might convince you to share Delia Smith's conviction that the human story embraces progress from evolution towards eventual unity with each other and with God?
4. Should politicians in the UK 'do God', or should matters of religious faith be left outside political debate?

RESOURCES

Delia Smith's biography on her website www.deliaonline.com.

Alastair Campbell's website, including his blog and a biography is at http://www.alastaircampbell.org/.

The book to which Alastair referred is his *The Happy Depressive: In pursuit of personal and political happiness* (Arrow, 2012).

One of Delia Smith's books on spirituality, *A Feast for Advent* (BRF, 2006) is still available, and she is writing more.